# CONCEIVE YOUR DREAMS

### AND GIVE BIRTH
### TO THE VISION
### OF YOUR HEART

PURPOSE • VISION • PASSION

## Howard Byrd

Hush Harbor Press
Charlotte NC USA

**Conceive Your Dreams**

And Give Birth to the Vision of Your Heart

ISBN: 978-0-692-52214-1

Published by Hush Harbor Press
Design and layout by Lighthouse24
Cover photo licensed from Masterfile

*To the love of my life, my wife Michelle. Thank you for helping me to see the true treasure in a woman. I never dreamed investing in one bag of M&M's® would bring me such joy.*

# Acknowledgements

To my wife and my children, Micah, Mikaela and William who put up with the late nights and short weekends to help me fulfill my calling.

To my mother, Loretta Byrd, who sacrificed so many of her own opportunities for the sake of her children.

To my father, Theodore Byrd, who taught me from the very beginning to respect and honor women.

To my sisters, Sharon, Karen and Keya, who gave so much frank and helpful insight into the psyche of today's woman.

# Contents

# CONCEIVE
# YOUR
# DREAMS

# Preface

EVERYONE DREAMS: the rich, poor, old and young. It is one of the few things we don't have to be taught. Sometimes dreams are the product of an active imagination or just a way to pass the time. However God has a more significant purpose for dreams. He uses them to give us a glimpse of what is possible through Him. Our thoughts are filled with things we desire to accomplish or become. Everything we see in the physical realm that was made by man began in the mind. We see the evidence of dreams in action in our everyday lives.

What we also see are the dreams that go unfinished. The fractured remains of a house that stands incomplete because the funds were exhausted. The business with the boarded windows and peeling paint devastated by poor planning, or the promising student who dropped out of school because of an unplanned pregnancy. If not put into proper perspective these images can cause you to be hesitant in pursuing your dreams and stop you short of your goals.

On an even greater scale are the dreams we never see; the visions that are aborted before they ever have an opportunity to fully develop. Hidden in the minds of people you meet every day are ideas that could solve major problems and be a blessing to millions of people, yet they are destined to stay locked in a mental vault because their owners fear failure more than they desire success. They never allow that seed thought to take root and grow, because to them the odds against success are overwhelming.

It is my prayer as you turn the pages of this book that you will become uncomfortable with where you are. I pray you will shake free from the chains of the past and grab hold of a cloud in the horizon of your destiny. God is waiting for you to start the dream he already sees as complete. Even if you have lost confidence in yourself, have faith in God. He is the one who inspired the dreams in you with an expectation that you will pursue them.

Through examples of God's divine guidance in women who desired physical conception, I will parallel how that same divine guidance can lead to the birth of your spiritual dream. In the physical world there is a process that leads to the actual birth. If for any reason there is a problem then that child may not be conceived or born. We will visit several women in various stages of conception to show how a missed step in the process will cause your dream not to be delivered or come to fruition. No matter what has happened in your past, God will revive and strengthen your vision. Just as those who were barren called out to Him and were rewarded, you will receive that same favor from God in your soul. The time is now—your barrenness will end and you will conceive your dreams and give birth to the vision of your heart.

# Introduction

ONCE, WHILE GATHERING TRASH in the house, I pulled a small basket out of the corner of the room. I noticed one of my children had missed the basket after they had finished eating some grapes. As I bent down to pick up the remnants of the branch, I marveled at how much it had changed. Earlier that week the same branch lay in the refrigerator tender, green and full of grapes. Just days later it was brown, stiff and drawn up like a withered hand. I didn't think about it again until later on that week when the Lord spoke to me through His word.

> I am the true vine and my Father is the gardener. He cuts off every branch in me that bears no fruit, while every branch that does bear fruit he prunes so that it will be even more fruitful. You are already clean because of the word I have spoken to you. Remain in me, and I will remain in you. No branch can bear fruit by itself; it must remain in the vine. Neither can you bear fruit unless you remain in me. I am the vine; you are the branches. If a man remains in me and I in him, he will bear much fruit; apart from me you can do nothing. If anyone does not remain in me, he is like a branch that is thrown away and

withers; such branches are picked up, thrown into the fire and burned. If you remain in me and my words remain in you, ask whatever you wish, and it will be given to you. This is to my Father's glory, that you bear much fruit, showing yourselves to be my disciples.

John 15:1-8

# Good Success

The branch was brown because it was no longer connected to the vine. It gave the appearance of being full of life for a few days but could not sustain its impressive facade. There is a point that you must be very clear on while pursuing your dreams: anything you produce that is not connected to God will not be able to sustain life. That is why Jesus said, "I am the vine and you are the branches." Many women in today's society have confused promotion with progress. Just because you appear to be successful to other people does not mean you have achieved real success. The only way to produce something that has a lasting effect in the kingdom of God is for it to be connected to God through a relationship with Jesus Christ. God differentiates success in Joshua, Chapter 1.

This Book of the Law shall not depart from your mouth, but you shall meditate in it day and night, that you might observe to do all that is written in it. For then you will make your way prosperous, and then you will have good success.

Joshua 1:8 (NKJV)

God specifically says "good success" which implies that there is bad success. No matter how many glass ceilings you break through or barriers you overcome to achieve a dream, if you do it outside of the will of God, it will always cost more than it was worth and leave you lifeless and unfruitful. The grapes my children enjoyed only lasted a short while, and they were also seedless, they had no way to produce more life. You have an opportunity to produce good fruit with seeds that will inspire others to fulfill their dreams. You will also be able to bear the pruning of the Father, stay connected to the vine, and produce more fruit.

> I am the true vine and my Father is the gardener. He cuts off every branch in me that bears no fruit, while every branch that does bear fruit he prunes so that it will be even more fruitful.
>
> John 15:1-2

That is why Jesus said, "Remain in me, and I will remain in you. No branch can bear fruit by itself; it must remain in the vine. Neither can you bear fruit unless you remain in me" (John 15:4). God knows you cannot produce good fruit on your own. Just as God will remove unproductive servants, He is committed to removing the dead branches from your life so you can produce more fruit. He is not trying to limit your dreams, He wants to liberate them.

> If you remain in me and my words remain in you, ask whatever you wish, and it will be given to you. This is to my Father's glory, that you bear much fruit, showing yourselves to be my disciples.
>
> John 15:7-8

## Looking Beyond the Surface

You may have had the experience of buying fruit because it looks good. You see a brightly colored strawberry or a shiny apple and succumb to its beauty, only to go home and find it was not as sweet as you thought or as juicy as you envisioned. The brightest strawberries are not always the sweetest and the shiny apples not always the most delicious. People may also fool you from a natural point of view. Many women have dressed themselves up appearing to be successful while hiding the bitterness that lies within. You can see it in the broken marriages of Hollywood's biggest female stars always seeking attention to mask the inner struggle for real fulfillment. Many women in the corporate arena who fought with great passion to reach the top of the mountain, realize only in hindsight, that it came with the price of a neglected spouse and wayward children. Good success has a price but it never neglects the intangibles. That is why any dream that you have that is good but not right for you must be cut away. Jesus tells us to count the cost before we begin building our vision within the kingdom (Luke 14:28). By staying connected to God the Father through Jesus Christ, you won't stray from your God-inspired dreams. And if you do, the gardener will be there to prune you.

Bearing fruit will require you to turn away from the standards of society. It will demand that you keep your eyes off the perceived success of those who don't follow God. Branches that bear much fruit must be willing to ignore the counsel of the ungodly. You must be willing to break free from the opinion of well-intentioned family members who advise you to play it safe. The only good fruit you will bear will be from the dreams that stir your spirit. The dreams that keep you awake at night and inspire you to righteous anger. God has given you His word as a manual for good success. His words are always there for you as you follow the Spirit of God in pursuit of your dreams.

> I have told you this so that my joy may be in you
> and that your joy may be complete.
>
> John 15:11

Stay connected to the Father and your dreams will certainly become a reality.

# Part I
# CONCEPTION

# CHAPTER ONE
# No More Miscarriage

A WOMB IS BEST SUITED to carry what it conceives when it is mature. Something so precious as a developing child in an immature womb is dangerous because it will often result in a miscarriage. In addition, a developing child always places harsh physical demands on its mother because she must provide all the nutrients for growth. That is why a woman is given special vitamins and eats constantly when she is pregnant.

With that in mind, you should take heed and develop your mind and spirit so that the strength you acquire through meditating in His word will allow you to carry what God places in your heart to term. Spiritual junk food won't do it; you must eat the word to have the strength to sustain yourselves as well as your dream, especially in the early stages when it is most vulnerable. Losing the vision of your dream at this stage can be difficult indeed because you feel the pain of losing something that never fully developed.

I recall an incident that occurred the day that my son was born that opened my eyes to this. I was in the maternity ward looking at all the newborns through the large picture window in the hallway. Another gentleman was standing there looking with me, and as we began to talk, I asked him which one of the babies belonged to him. "My wife had a miscarriage," he replied. At first I was at a loss for words.

What do you say to those who have just lost something so precious to them even though they have never seen it? I don't know what caused it, or if this had happened to his wife before. Regardless, I am sure that the pain would not have been any different. Fortunately, God gave me an encouraging word for him to give him hope in the future:

> Worship the lord your God, and his blessing will be on your food and water. I will take sick ones from among you and none of you will miscarry or be barren in the land.
>
> Exodus 23:25-26

God also has an encouraging word for you concerning the vision you may have previously miscarried. This time your conception will survive and be a blessing that will uplift and expand His kingdom.

> ...being confident in this, that he who began a good work in you will carry it on to completion until the day of Christ Jesus.
>
> Philippians 1:6

## Overcoming Fear

The reason you must encourage yourself in the Lord is that miscarried dreams are one of the main causes of the fear to try again. When your expectations are crushed by the loss of something that never fully developed, you have a tendency to play it safe and never try again. Fear of failure becomes a type of spiritual birth control. You may begin to say things like "I will just adopt someone else's vision that has already developed." Many of you may already be living someone else's dream.

You may have suffered through so many miscarriages of your dream that you have decided to give up because somehow you have concluded that God cannot use you because your dream has not flourished as others have. The truth of the matter is you will never find fulfillment in the dreams of others while yours slowly dies. God has resurrecting power and is able to give you the strength to endure until the end. God is waiting for you to expose the very thing you buried in your heart, because of fear, doubt, and unbelief, so that He can give it new life.

Do not give up if you have miscarried your dreams. Do not quit because you failed once before when you tried to do something great for the kingdom of God. If you want to conceive and give birth to the things of God you cannot stand around hoping it will happen. You must believe that it must happen and get busy moving toward your goal.

In the childbirth process, if you and your spouse want to conceive a child you can talk about it until you turn blue. You can read all the manuals of conception and you can even go to seminars and workshops on conception. All of these things are good but if you and your spouse don't work at it, your conception will never happen. Trust God and work with Him to conceive the vision for your life.

# CHAPTER TWO
# The Elements of Conception

IN MARK, CHAPTER 4, Jesus was teaching on the parable of the sower. This is the cornerstone example of what God desires for His children.

> Listen! A farmer went out to sow his seed. As he was scattering the seed, some fell along the path, and the birds came and ate it up. Some fell on rocky places, where it did not have much soil. It sprang up quickly, because the soil was shallow. But when the sun came up, the plants were scorched, and they withered because they had no root. Other seed fell among thorns, which grew up and choked the plants, so they did not bear grain. Still other seed fell on good soil. It came up, grew and produced a crop, multiplying thirty, sixty or even a hundred times. Then Jesus said, 'He who has ears to hear, let him hear.'
>
> Mark 4:3-9

Jesus teaches that a farmer went out to sow seed, and the seed landed in four different places: along the path, on rocky places, among thorns, and on good soil. The seed's ability to produce a crop was based on the place it landed when it was scattered. Later when Jesus and His disciples were alone they asked Him why he spoke in parables to religious leaders but explained the parables to them in private. Jesus' answer gave an important insight on how God wants you to receive his instruction on pursuing your dreams. He said to them:

> The secret of the kingdom of God has been given to you. But to those on the outside everything is said in parables so that, they may be ever seeing but never perceiving, and ever hearing but never understanding; otherwise they might turn and be forgiven!
>
> Mark 4:11-12

## Seeking God for Revelation

God wants to reveal His will for your life, but He wants you to seek it through Him. Then when you discover it, you will follow through with your plans because you know you have heard from God. In Mark 4:14 Jesus said, "The farmer sows the word". God wants to sow His word into your life. He wants to reveal His plan and His wisdom to you by His word. When seeking to conceive a dream and give birth to a vision, you must do so in light of God's word. This will ensure that what you desire to accomplish is within God's plan for your life. When you have a dream, it can be defined as a visionary creation of the imagination or a strongly desired goal or purpose. When your dream becomes a vision, it is from a supernatural encounter with God that conveys a revelation. The plan is literally unveiled to your senses from something immaterial. You move from conception to a vision to giving birth by the supernatural power of God that is in you.

Every natural conception involves some key elements that must be in place for it to fully develop. If any of these elements are omitted, what is conceived will not survive. This also holds true in the realm of the spirit. By having the word of God as the key element in the conception of your dreams, you have the foundation for success. To properly appreciate this principle, you must have a more thorough understanding of the root word *ceive*.

The word *ceive* is derived from the Latin word *capere*, which is defined as to *take hold of*, *to grasp* or *to seize*. Jesus explained to His disciples that the seed that was *ceived* or *captured* in the parable was the word of God. There are two types of words that God will sow into your life. The first type of word is the Greek word *logos*. Simply stated, this is the expression of what God has already said. The Bible is the logos of God. This word is for everyone and is to be used to help you walk in the principles and precepts God has commanded all men to operate by. The other type of word is the Greek word *rhema*; this is what God is saying to you now. Every rhema word is not for everyone, but for the individual(s) it was revealed to. This is the word Satan attacks with the most zeal because he knows if you receive it he is powerless in his attempt to defeat you.

There are many examples in the Bible of individuals receiving a word from God. Abraham, Moses, Joshua, David and many others were given specific definitive instructions from God. The Apostle Paul says in Romans 10:17, "So then faith comes by hearing and hearing by the (rhema) word of God." You can receive revelation from God by both types of word, but your destiny lies in God's *rhema* word for your life.

Seed will not be profitable unless it is planted in good ground. No matter how much you like apples, holding apple seeds in your hand will not enable them to become apple trees. If you want them to produce you must plant them in the proper soil. The same principle holds true when you are trying to conceive your dream. God's word is always good, but in order to get maximum results it must be received into a willing mind. In the parable of the sower, the four places the seed landed, along the path, on the rocky place, among thorns and on good soil all represent the way people receive the word of God. We could then say your mind and your spirit are the *soil* or *womb* for the word. The condition of that womb determines the success of the word that was planted. To *receive* means to acquire what is released. Jesus knew that all people were not ready to receive his word.

## The Path

Jesus first described the seed that fell along the path (Mark 4:15). This is the word that was received, but only on the surface. This person has no relationship with God, which is why Satan is able to steal the word with relative ease. No real conception takes place and the seed is not able to produce. A poor attitude towards God or the person releasing His word can hinder you from receiving the word.

## The Rocky Place

Jesus then described the seed that fell on the rocky place. In the Middle East, there are many places that have a thin layer of earth that covers solid stone. The seed that falls germinates and even has shallow roots. As the days grow hot, though, and the roots are unable to dig deeper, the sun scorches them and they wither and die. This is the person who has a casual relationship with God. They may have been inspired by a fiery Sunday morning sermon but never get deeply rooted in the word of God. When things get uncomfortable, they give up on God and their dream. A casual relationship with God never produces good fruit. If you expect to realize your dreams, your spiritual roots must go deeper than the surface.

## Thorns and Weeds

Wherever you have soil there is always the potential for weeds and undesirable plants. These plants must be removed or they can steal the nutrients from the desired crop that was purposely planted. If you take the highest quality seed and plant it in rich soil then the seed will germinate and grow. But if you don't remove the weeds and undesired plants they will choke the life out of the plant and destroy the potential harvest. Any selfish ambition will act as spiritual weeds to what God inspires in you. That is one of the ways you will know that what you desire is from God. He would never inspire you to do anything that does not benefit other people. If you allow greed, jealousy or any other negative trait to dominate your thoughts and emotions, you will end up killing your dream.

## Don't Make Your Problems Special

You must also be aware that just because God gives you a dream, does not guarantee that fulfilling that dream will be easy to accomplish. You may have received the word of God for your life—you may have acquired it. But to *conceive* means to take hold of and grasp it. In fact, your God-inspired dreams will cause the enemy to mobilize his forces against you. He will do everything in his power to magnify your problems. He is afraid of what God has placed in you and he knows he has no authority to stop you. The enemy will do his best to try to make you feel as if you are the only one going through trials in pursuit of your dream. He will bring people into your midst whose sole purpose is to try to remove the word of God from you thereby destroying your faith.

> Therefore let that abide in you which you heard from the beginning. If what you heard from the beginning abides in you, you also will abide in the Son and in the Father. And this is the promise that He has promised us – eternal life. These things I have written to you concerning those who try to **deceive** you. But the anointing which you have received from Him abides in you, and you do not need that anyone teach you; but the same anointing teaches you concerning all things, and is true, and is not a lie, just as it has taught you, you will abide in Him.
>
> 1 John 2:24-27 (NKJV)

The message heard from the beginning was the Gospel of the kingdom and that God wants His Spirit to dwell in man to guide him in the way that he should go. The enemy will send people into your life to try and *deceive* you. To deceive means to remove what has been received or conceived. The word of God says He has given you the *anointing,* or *power* of God, and you do not need any man to teach what is contrary to that word. You have to keep your mind on the task at hand, knowing God has given you the ability to withstand your troubles.

> No temptation has seized you except what is **common** to man. And God is faithful; he will not let you be tempted beyond what you can bear. But when you are tempted, he will also provide a way out so that you can stand up under it.
>
> 1 Corinthians 10:13

You must remember your troubles are not special. You are not the only one with bills; you are not the only single mother, or the only one trying to pursue a dream without a college degree. All the cares of this world may seem too much to handle, but remember, "God is faithful". He has given you the power to overcome all obstacles through a relationship with Jesus Christ.

> For everyone born of God overcomes the world. This is the victory that has overcome the world, even our faith. Who is it that overcomes the world? Only he who believes that Jesus is the Son of God.
>
> I John 5:4-5

## Becoming Good Ground

Everyone who has the desire to fulfill the will of God in his or her lives has the potential to be good soil. By allowing the dream that God places in your heart to dominate your subconscious thoughts, you are grooming yourself for greatness.

> Still other seed fell on good soil. It came up, grew and produced a crop, multiplying thirty, sixty, or even a hundred times.
>
> Mark 4:8

God desires to reveal the riches of his plans for you. When you open your spirit to Him, He will begin to show you the mystery of the glory of your future. Good soil is found in the mind of a willing and obedient servant of God. Good soil is found in a woman who is full of love and faith. Good soil is found in the heart of those who are able to forgive. You cannot expect to live your dream if you cloud your mind with circumstances of the day. To become good ground for a *rhema* word from God you must reaffirm your connection to the Spirit of God through your relationship with Jesus. Because of Jesus, God's Spirit is not only with you, but also in you and God has promised to reveal your future. You have a right to receive wisdom from God.

> We do, however, speak a message of wisdom among the mature, but not the wisdom of this age or of the rulers of this age, who are coming to nothing. No, we speak of God's secret wisdom that has been hidden and that God has destined for our glory before time began. None of the rulers of this age understood it, for if they had they would not have crucified the Lord of glory. However as it is written: 'No eye has seen

no ear has heard no mind has conceived what
God has prepared for those who love him.' but
God has revealed it to us by his Spirit. The Spirit
searches all things, even the deep things of God.
For who among men knows the thoughts of a
man except the man's spirit within him? In the
same way no one knows the thoughts of God
except the spirit of God. We have not received
the spirit of the world but the Spirit who is from
God, that we may understand what God has
freely given us.

1 Corinthians 2:6-12

To become good soil and conceive your dream you must
think like Jesus thought, and that requires a desire to walk
according to the spirit. As a believer you are given the right
and the ability to walk in the wisdom of God.

For who has known the mind of the Lord that he
may instruct him? But we have the mind of Christ.

1 Corinthians 2:16

Just as a seed that has been planted in good soil
germinates and produces a crop, you must receive a word
for your life that takes hold in your spiritual womb. Once
that occurs you are ready to begin the time of growth and
preparation of or the delivery of your vision.

# CHAPTER THREE
# Is Anything Too Hard
# For The Lord?

WE SOMETIMES NEED to be reminded of the immeasurable power of God. He has no need to hire a personal trainer to get in shape to perform a miracle for you. God is a God of faith; it is the only way He operates. When He speaks something it must happen because His word cannot return to him without accomplishing its purpose. Our finite minds find it difficult to comprehend his infinite power. We can see a situation as impossible but God sees it as an "easy thing" (2 Kings 3:18).

Perhaps you have been waiting on the conception of your dream for quite some time and your faith is beginning to fade. This is a common problem of our human frailty. I have heard many women say, "If it has not happened yet it never will," even if they are in the prime of life. The odds may seem stacked against you and you can no longer see a clear path to victory. You need to understand that every great vision comes to a point where natural human ability can no longer support what God has placed in your future. His vision for you is always bigger than what you can do in your own strength. It is in these situations that God can prove His promises to us and exercise his power, so those who serve Him can glorify Him. If your dream seems impossible to you this is a perfect time for you to pray and simply wait. Whatever you ask for, God is willing to give you more.

> Now to him who is able to do immeasurably more than all we ask or imagine, according to his power that is at work within us.
>
> Ephesians 3:20

In the book of Genesis Chapter 12 we find that God called Abram and his wife Sarai out of Ur of the Chaldeans.

> The Lord had said to Abram, 'Leave your country, your people and your father's household and go to a land I will show you. I will make you a great nation and will bless you; I will make your name great and you will be a blessing. I will bless those who bless you and whoever curses you I will curse; and all the peoples on the earth will be blessed through you.'
>
> Genesis 12:1-3

## It Is Never Too Late

There was however a challenge that Abram and Sarai faced. They were old and had probably given up on the idea of having children when God told Abram he was going to be a great nation. They were obedient and moved when they heard from God, but the challenges that lay ahead would cause both of them to stretch their faith. During the next several years Sarai would have to endure the frustration and shame of her barrenness. In ancient times, as in many cultures today, a woman who did not bear children was often considered cursed. Sarai was a beautiful woman who was faithful to her husband. She knew he loved her despite the fact she did not bear him children. During their journey together she would be asked to lie for Him, and even be put in harm's way because Abram feared for his own life. In all this time God did not speak directly to her. She was relying on that which her husband was hearing from God.

> After this the word of the Lord came to Abram in a vision: 'Do not be afraid, Abram. I am your shield, your very great reward.' But Abram said, 'O Sovereign Lord, what can you give me since I remain childless and the one who will inherit my estate is Eliezer of Damascus?' And Abram said 'You have given me no children; so a servant in my household will be my heir.' Then the word of the Lord came to him: 'This man will not be your heir, but a son coming from your own body will be your heir.'
>
> Genesis 15:1-4

The Bible says Abram believed God and it was credited to him as righteousness. But what about Sarai? How could she interpret what God had spoken to Abram? If he told her what God said, she could say that the child would come from Abram but that did not mean the Lord would allow her to be the mother. Her doubts began to get the best of her as time went on.

> Now Sarai Abram's wife had borne him no children. But she had a maidservant named Hagar; so she said to Abram 'The Lord has kept

me from having children. Go, sleep with my maidservant; perhaps I can build my family through her.'

Genesis 16:1-2

## Don't Compromise the Vision

This may seem like a bizarre suggestion for a wife to give to her husband, but it was a common practice in the ancient world. However, this was a great error on the part of Sarai because you can never live God's destiny for your life through someone else. Abram had relations with Hagar and she did become pregnant and Sarai despised her because of it. The Bible does not tell us how long they were together or how long it took her to become pregnant. What we do know is that Abram became very attached to Hagar. When you do things out of desperation because of internal or external pressure, there is a good chance they may come back to mock you.

Almost everyone can identify with Sarai on some level. The great dream in your spiritual womb is constantly pulling on your faith. We have all given into our fears at some point in our life. There may be something you have encouraged to come about, hoping it would help your situation and now it is a constant reminder of your failure and impatience. Ishmael, the son born to Abram and Hagar, was Sarai's reminder, and eventually she had to take drastic measures to correct the situation.

When Abram was 99 years old, the Lord appeared to him and affirmed his promise that he would make him a great nation. He established the covenant of circumcision for all the males born in his family as well. But another important thing God did was change Abram's name to Abraham, which means father of multitudes. He also changed Sarai's name to Sarah, which means princess. God confirmed his intent by telling Abraham that Sarah would be the mother of the heir of promise. Their names were changed so they would begin to speak what God had promised. This was so overwhelming to Abraham that he laughed at the thought of it and asked God to let Ishmael be the heir. He could not believe at the age 99 and Sarah at 90 that they would have a child together. The Lord visited Abraham once again by sending three visitors to his household. They gave him the promise that the child would be born within a year.

> Then the Lord said, 'I will surely return to you about this time next year, and Sarah your wife will have a son.' Now Sarah was listening at the entrance of the tent which was behind him. Abraham and Sarah were already old and well advanced in years, and Sarah was past the age of childbearing. So Sarah laughed to herself and thought, 'After I am worn out and my master is old, will I now have this pleasure?' Then the Lord said to Abraham, 'Why did Sarah laugh and say, 'Will I really have a child now that I am old?' Is anything too hard for the Lord? I will return to you at the appointed time and Sarah will have a son,' Sarah was afraid so she lied and said 'I did not laugh' But he said 'Yes you did laugh.'
>
> Genesis 18:10-15

# God Is Able

God asked Abraham a question that everyone who desires to accomplish a great dream has to answer "Is anything too hard for the Lord?" Sarah had to answer the same question. God had put them in a position where only He could empower them to conceive. Sarah had been through menopause and Abraham was too old to do anything if she had not been. They both had to rely on their faith to conceive this promised child, and you will have to rely on your faith to conceive your dream. Faith does not believe God can do anything; faith is being certain God will do what He has committed Himself to do. When you pray to conceive God's vision for your life you must believe He is able to do it through you. There will always be challenges to your faith that may cause you to question the viability of your vision. You will not be able to move forward until you can answer the question, "Is anything too hard for the Lord?"

Joseph had to answer that question in a pit, in slavery, and in prison. Moses answered it before the Red Sea would part and Joshua before the sun stood still so that he could win the battle. And Esther answered it before she went before the king without being summoned, which could have been a death sentence. David gave an answer on the way to meet Goliath. Daniel answered in the darkness of a lion's den. And the Hebrew boys answered on their way to the fiery furnace. All of them had to believe God when they knew their natural ability would not be enough.

These are great examples, but the fact remains you have to believe God for yourself. Before you proceed any further with your vision, you must purpose in your heart that there is not anything that is too hard for God. Your faith in God is the key to your success.

> With man this is impossible, but not with God; all things are possible with God.
>
> Mark 10:27

## Think Big

If the dream you have for your life can be accomplished without supernatural assistance, it is not big enough. Envision something that will pull on your faith and present it to God. He has a much better promise than your *Ishmael* can bring you because that is limited to your flesh.

> By faith Sarah herself also received strength to conceive seed, and she bore a child when she was past the age, because she judged Him faithful who had promised.
>
> Hebrews 11:11

God has an *Isaac* for your life, a promised child conceived in your soul. This promise will bring you a new understanding of God's love and provision. Just as Sarah had to send Ishmael away after he began to mock her son, you will have to cast out what you have produced in your natural ability. However you will not send Ishmael away until Isaac is conceived. As you will soon understand the battle between your spiritual fulfillment and your desires of the flesh will be the biggest and most difficult you will face.

# Part II
# GESTATION

# CHAPTER FOUR
# Two Nations Are in Your Womb

MANY OF US THRIVE on competition, the challenge to prove we are better, smarter, faster, and wealthier than anyone else. No true competitor is ever satisfied with coming in second. I often get a good laugh when I see movie stars and musicians proclaim, "It was an honor just to be nominated." The truth of the matter is they may love acting or music, but once they are nominated they want to win. I have also heard it said no one wins at war. If that were the case no one would surrender. There are casualties on both sides, but only one side admits defeat.

## The Battle Lines

Every believer is at war and there is a constant battle that rages within. The prize is your soul and the two adversaries are your spirit and your flesh. Your spirit is recreated when you accept Jesus Christ as Savior. You have a guarantee that your spirit no longer has to fight the temptation of sin, because your recreated spirit is connected to God. Your flesh is unchanged and will remain that way until the resurrection. That is why your body still craves the things it always has and enjoys sin. Your flesh only seeks to please itself. Your body does not care if you are on a diet, if it wants cake it will make demands for cake. If you were delivered from sexual sin your body still wants to do what it used to do. Your spirit and your flesh are at war with each other to control the way you think. They both want control over your soul. That is how one of them will win the war for dominance in your life. How you think will determine whether you will have pie or salad. It will decide if you will control your passions or give into your desire for pleasure. God knows the struggles you will face between a recreated spirit and a lustful body, and that is why we are told:

> Therefore I urge you brothers, in view of God's mercy to offer your bodies as living sacrifices, holy and pleasing to God—this is your spiritual act of worship. Do not conform any longer to the pattern of this world, but be transformed by the renewing of your mind. Then you will able to test and approve what God's will is—his good, pleasing and perfect will.
>
> Romans 12:1-2

Your mind was put into a strange position when you were born again; it still remembers how to do all the evil you once enjoyed. However, it has never before been so prepared to learn the perfect will of God. Your soul is made up of your mind, your will, and your emotions. Your will is your decision-maker and it is influenced by your thoughts and emotions. You will decide whether your flesh or your spirit will win the allegiance of your mind. That's why Paul wrote:

> Finally, brothers, whatever is true, whatever is noble, whatever is right, whatever is pure,

whatever is lovely, whatever is admirable—if anything is excellent or praiseworthy-think about such things.

Philippians 4:8

## Discipline Is a Product of the Will

It is important for you to discipline your mind to think about the things that matter to God. Philippians 2:5 says that our attitude should be the same as Christ's. You may be surprised to know that your will and God's will don't have to be the same. It is however important that you are willing to submit your obedience to God. You may be wondering how you can be obedient as long as your will is not the same as that of God's. The answer lies in the Garden of Gethsemane; Jesus had to deal with this issue before He could complete His assignment.

> Then he said to them, (Peter, James and John) 'My soul is overwhelmed with sorrow to the point of death. Stay here and keep watch with me' Going a little farther, he fell with his face to the ground and prayed, 'My Father, if it is possible, may this cup be taken from me. Yet not as I will, but as you will.'
>
> Matthew 26:38-39

We can see from this passage that Jesus the Christ had to be willing to submit His will to God the Father in order to complete his assignment. His body was weary and did not want to endure the hardship it was going to face. He had to make up his mind that he would be obedient.

Who, being in the very nature of God, did not consider equality with God something to be grasped, but made himself nothing taking the very nature of a servant, being made in human likeness. And being found in appearance as a man, he humbled himself and became obedient to death – even death on a cross! Therefore God exalted him to the highest place and gave him the name that is above every name, that at the name of Jesus every knee shall bow in heaven and on earth and under the earth, and every tongue shall confess that Jesus Christ is Lord to the glory of God the Father.

Philippians 2:6-11

If you are going to fulfill the dream that God has given you for your life you must make up in your mind that you will be obedient. Your body will not volunteer itself to be used by God; you must command it to be obedient. When you do this you will put yourself in position to be propelled by God into your destiny.

In Genesis Chapter 24 we find that as Abraham is advancing in years, he becomes very concerned about finding a proper wife for his son Isaac. He made one of his trusted servants swear an oath that he would not find a wife from among the Canaanites where Abraham was dwelling. The servant was commanded to go back to Ur of the Chaldeans where Abraham's family was from. It was a common practice in ancient times to marry someone in the extended family in order to avoid intermingling with other nations. The servant obeyed and brought back Rebekah, a relative of Abraham's. As they arrived in Canaan, Rebekah dismounted her camel, and when she saw Isaac she placed a veil over her face as a sign that she was willing to become his wife. She and Isaac were married soon after, which was a comfort to Isaac because he had recently lost his mother.

Isaac and Rebekah were truly in love, and enjoyed their life together. However, there was one major problem. After nineteen years of marriage Rebekah had not conceived any children. Isaac could see the disappointment in his wife year after year and it began to trouble him. Rebekah had to exercise restraint; it is quite possible she was tempted to do what Sarah did and produce a child by a surrogate mother. Isaac finally had had enough and sought the Lord on behalf of his wife.

> Isaac prayed to the Lord on behalf of his wife, because she was barren. The Lord answered his prayer and Rebekah became pregnant.
>
> Genesis 25:21

## The Battle Within

Rebekah and Isaac were on their way to manifesting the promise the Lord had given to Abraham. Rebekah no longer had to hold her head in shame because of her barren womb. As her pregnancy progressed she began to feel a struggle in her womb. She then did what we should all do when we find ourselves in a similar situation; she sought God to find an answer.

> The babies jostled within her, and she said, 'Why is this happening to me?' So she went to inquire

of the Lord. The Lord said to her 'Two nations
are in your womb, and two peoples from within
you will be separated; one people will be
stronger than the other, and older will serve the
younger.'

Genesis 25:22-23

When Rebekah conceived after being barren for nearly
twenty years, she may have thought she would have at the
very least an uneventful pregnancy. It may have come as a
shock to her that such a battle raged within her womb. You
may experience the same thing in your own situation. When
you receive a *rhema* word from God concerning your
destiny, there will be a decision you will have to confront.
You will have to decide whether to follow the spiritual path
to your vision or to produce an inferior result through your
flesh. Remember when Rebekah sought God, He not only
gave her an answer but also made a declaration. Two
nations were in her womb, two forces battling for position
and they would be separated. God also declared that the
older would serve the younger. This was contrary to the
culture where the oldest son was given twice the amount of
inheritance as any additional sons. Surely God would not
have him to serve the younger sibling.

From this passage of scripture, you can see that God is
not bound by our culture or our way of reasoning. Just as
Rebekah's children battled within her, your flesh and your
spirit will battle for control of your *soul* (your mind, will,
and emotions). To fulfill the calling that God has for your
life, your spirit must prevail. There is only room for one
ruler in your life, and you are the one who will choose. If

you choose the flesh, your destiny is vulnerable to the attack of the enemy.

> Like a city whose walls are broken down is a man who lacks self-control.
>
> > Proverbs 25:28

If you do not exercise self-control, the wall that guards your mind is broken down and can be easily attacked by the enemy. You will begin to succumb to the desire to please your flesh and that can lead to the destruction of your vision.

> When the time came for her to give birth, there were twin boys in her womb. The first to come out was red, and his whole body was like a hairy garment; so they named him Esau (hairy). After this, his brother came out with his hand grasping Esau's heel; so he was named Jacob (he grasped the heel) Isaac was sixty years old when Rebekah gave birth to them.
>
> > Genesis 25:24-26

## The Consequences of Serving the Flesh

The story continues that the boys grew up and Esau became a skilled hunter, while Jacob stayed around the tents. One day, a major flaw in Esau's character allowed poor judgment to break through the walls that guarded his mind. After a long day of hunting, Esau saw Jacob cooking stew and asked to share in the meal because he was worn down. Jacob, being a person of deception, demanded that Esau sell his birthright, which gave him a double portion of his father's inheritance: for what—for a bowl of stew! What makes the incident even more troubling is that Jacob did not even have to convince Esau to do it. Esau let his flesh rule and made a very costly decision, allowing the discomfort of his flesh to have more value to him than the impending day of his blessing and inheritance.

You may recall a situation in which you have acted in a similar fashion. Your flesh does not consider the consequences in the same way that your spirit does. That is why you must exercise your will to overcome the desires of your flesh. From this incident we can see God's fore-knowledge of Esau's character flaw and the reason for His declaration to Rebekah.

In the eastern culture, the father's blessing is extremely important. Isaac was not aware of the deal that had been struck between his sons. As he began to age, his health declined and he called for his favored son Esau and said,

> I am now an old man and don't know the day of my death. Now get your weapons—your quiver and your bow—and go out to hunt some wild game for me. Prepare me the kind of tasty food I like and bring it to me to eat, so that I may bless you before I die.
>
> Genesis 27:2-4

Rebekah was listening and plotted with Jacob to deceive her nearly blind husband, and have her favored son receive the blessing instead of Esau. She should have known that she did not have to be manipulative for Jacob to be blessed. God had promised that the older would serve the younger.

They successfully fooled Isaac and Jacob received the blessing of the firstborn. In doing so, even more animosity grew between the two brothers, so much so that Jacob had to leave home because his brother was planning to kill him after their father's death.

When God had promised Rebekah the older child will serve the younger and the younger would be the stronger nation and would rule over the older, she believed Him. She then allowed her fear to overcome her confidence in God's promise. God's desire is that your spirit should rule over your flesh, and He has given every believer the authority to live this way. It is your responsibility to make the decision to live by the spirit.

Just as in Rebekah's situation, two nations are in your womb. They are jostling for control and the elder will serve the younger. You have already learned that your mind must be renewed because this is the prize that your spirit and your flesh are fighting for. When you receive Christ as Savior, the only part of you that is immediately set free from sin is your spirit. Remember that your soul (your mind, will, and emotions) is still being renewed and your body (flesh) will not be renewed until the resurrection. Paul wrote:

> Therefore, if anyone is in Christ, he is a new creation; the old has gone and the new has come.
>
> 2 Corinthians 5:17

Paul is saying that your fallen, dead spirit is now gone and you have a new recreated spirit. If your spirit is new, it is younger than your sinful flesh. So now the older flesh is to serve the younger spirit, because the renewed mind has decided to live by the spirit. That is why after an encounter with God, Jacob, whose name means "deceiver," became "Israel," which means "prince of God." That experience with God enabled him to focus on changing the way he thinks and receive a greater measure of God's promise on his life.

You must continue to fight for control of your mind even after you receive Christ as Savior. God will not override your authority to control your will. Your flesh will continue to scream for attention and attempt to fulfill ungodly desires that will threaten the success of your vision. Paul writes in Galatians 5:16-18:

> So I say live by the Spirit and you will not gratify the desires of the sinful nature (flesh). For the sinful nature desires what is contrary to the Spirit and the Spirit what is contrary to the sinful nature. They are in conflict with each other, so you do not do what you want. But if you are lead by the Spirit you are not under the law.

Paul was speaking about a conflict between your spirit which is indwelled by the Holy Spirit and your flesh. It is your spirit and flesh that are in conflict with one another as witnessed later in Paul's exhortation. He concludes that the sinful desires of your flesh are contrary to the desires of your recreated spirit. Therefore the warfare is not with you and the Spirit of God, but within you.

> The acts of the sinful nature are obvious; sexual immorality, impurity and debauchery; idolatry and witchcraft; having discord, jealousy, fits of

rage, selfish ambition, dissentions, factions and envy; drunkenness, orgies and the like. I warn you as I did before that those who live like this will not inherit the kingdom of God.

Galatians 5:19-21

Paul gives a detailed description of the type of appetite the sinful nature has. Our flesh only seeks to please itself and does not care who is harmed along the way. God's vision for your life would never involve destroying yourself or others. Paul continues in Galatians 5:22-23:

> But the fruit of the Spirit is love, joy, peace, patience, kindness, goodness, faithfulness, gentleness and self-control. Against such things there is no law.

## God Is Not At War, You Are

The Holy Spirit is God, and therefore, He would not have conflict with the desires of the flesh. This, in my observation, would indicate the fruit that we produce is a product of our lives being led by our spirit, which is indwelled by the Spirit of God. The conflict is in us, not in God. Your flesh is vulnerable to your own sinful desires and the influence of wicked spiritual forces of Satan's kingdom.

> For we do not wrestle against flesh and blood but against principalities, against powers, against rulers of the darkness of this age, against spiritual host in heavenly places.

Ephesians 6:12 (NKJV)

Paul did not say we have wrestled, he said we wrestle. That means the battle is continuous. Your vision will only be realized if you are willing to fight for it. Always keep in mind that two nations are in your womb. When you decide to live by the spirit, you are on your way to victory, and the flesh that you need to function on this earth will have no choice but to serve your spirit. This world may promise quick success and a life of ease, but choosing to live by the flesh will lead to the destruction of your God-ordained purpose.

> Do not love the world or anything in the world. If anyone loves the world the love of the Father is not in him. For everything in the world –the cravings of the sinful man, the lust of his eyes and the boasting of what he has and does— comes not from the Father but from the world. The world and its desires pass away but the man who does the will of God lives forever.
>
> 1 John 2:15-17

God has given you an eternal purpose. Decide today to live and be led by the Spirit of God to conceive and give birth to your dream.

# CHAPTER FIVE
## Divine Delays

MOST PEOPLE HAVE HEARD the expression "good things come to those who wait." Here in the United States, the value of that statement has lost quite a bit of its meaning. In most areas of our lives we don't want to wait for anything. We have fast food, instant film development, microwave ovens, and the list goes on. We have lost sight of the value in completing a process to reach a goal. If things do not happen right away, we have a tendency to think something has gone wrong. The things we must work for to achieve or acquire, we tend to protect. Someone who has lived in a cramped apartment for ten years with three children will usually have a greater appreciation when they finally get a breakthrough and are able to purchase their own home.

In years past, I used to purchase a copy of *Forbes®* list of the four hundred wealthiest Americans. I discovered there was a profound difference between those who had to work for their money and those who inherited money. Those individuals who established their fortune through hard work usually appreciated and protected it. They were also more inclined to use the wealth to help others. Many of their descendants were in bitter court battles over wealth they had no part in earning. They did not appreciate the effort it took to obtain the wealth and were being impatient about receiving what they considered to be their piece of the inheritance pie.

## The Divine Timetable

You need to understand that God is not on our timetable. When God purposes something to be done, He has already determined the time frame in which it will be completed. Isaiah 46:9-10 says:

> Remember the former things, those of long ago; I am God and there is no other; I am God and there is none like me. I make known the end from the beginning, from ancient times, what is to come. I say: My purpose will stand, and I will do what I please.

Even when we are disobedient to the perfect will of God, He works it into His permissive will so that the assignment He has given you will still be accomplished. Ecclesiastes 3:1 says:

> There is a time for everything, and a season for every activity under heaven.

Patience is a quality that all believers should seek to build in their lives. It is a necessary attribute when you are pursuing a dream. No one enjoys delayed gratification, but the ability to wait on what is best instead of forcing something out that is half-baked is what sometimes separates the champion from the runner-up. Your faith in what God is doing in your life is the foundation for the patience you will develop while moving towards the manifestation of your vision. There will be obstacles to overcome and trials to endure. Every time you are faithful enough to maintain your position in the face of the challenges you encounter, you move up to a new level of maturity. James 1:2-4 says:

> Consider it pure joy, my brothers, whenever you face trials of many kinds, because the testing of your faith develops perseverance. Perseverance must finish it work that you may be mature and complete not lacking anything.

Perseverance is a counterpart to patience. Your dream must become so valuable to you that you are willing to endure hardship to achieve it. You must be prepared to fight, and when you cannot move forward, stand your ground until you receive your breakthrough. Remember the seed that fell on the rocky place could not endure the heat of the day and withered because its roots were not deep enough. You must allow the word of the Lord concerning your vision to be deeply imbedded in your soul, because there will be delays on the way to your destiny.

One of the greatest love stories of the Bible is that of Jacob and Rachel. Rebekah had persuaded Jacob to go to her brother, Laban's, house after he had taken his brothers birthright, because she knew Esau might kill Jacob after their father Isaac died. After traveling to Paddan Aram, Jacob met up with some herdsman who knew of Rebekah's brother. While he was standing there with them he had his first glimpse of Rachel. Genesis 29:9-15 says:

While he was still talking with them, Rachel came to water her father's sheep, for she was a shepherdess. When Jacob saw Rachel daughter of Laban, his mother's brother, and Laban's sheep, he went over and rolled the stone away from the mouth of the well and watered his uncle's sheep. Then Jacob kissed Rachel and began to weep aloud. He had told Rachel that he was a relative of her father and a son of Rebekah. So she ran and told her father. As soon as Laban heard the news about Jacob, his sister's son, he hurried to meet him. He embraced him and kissed him and brought him into his home, and there Jacob told him all these things. Then Laban said to him 'You are my own flesh and blood.'

Laban liked having Jacob around, and after a month he offered him the opportunity to stay on a permanent basis. He told Jacob he did not want him to work without compensation and ask him what he thought his wages should be. Genesis 29:16-20 says:

Now Laban had two daughters; the name of the older was Leah, and the name of the younger was Rachel. Leah had weak eyes, but Rachel was lovely in form and was beautiful. Jacob was in love and said, 'I'll work for you for seven years in return for your younger daughter Rachel.' Laban said, 'It is better that I give her to you than to some other man. Stay here with me.' So Jacob served for seven years to get Rachel, but it seemed like only a few days to him because of his love for her.

It may come to some a shock that Jacob would offer to serve seven years to marry a woman he had just met. However, in the ancient world a man, was expected to offer a dowry or substantial gift to the father of his bride-to-be. Jacob had come with nothing so his seven years of labor served as his dowry. The key element in that passage is that the time seemed like only a few days. The man had fallen madly in love in less than a month. Don't think that Rachel did not take notice of his devotion. Her anticipation was probably just as great as Jacob's was. She never heard him complain about the price he paid to get her and finally the day came for his reward. Genesis 29:21-30 says:

> Then Jacob said to Laban, 'Give me my wife. My time is completed and I want to lie with her.' So Laban brought together all of the people of the place and gave a feast. But when evening came, he took his daughter Leah and gave her to Jacob and Jacob lay with her. And Laban gave his servant girl Zilpah to his daughter as her maidservant. When morning came, there was Leah! So Jacob said to Laban, 'What is this you have done to me? I served you for Rachel, didn't I? Why have you deceived me?' Laban replied, 'It is not our custom here to give the younger daughter in marriage before the older one. Finish the bridal week; then we will give you the younger one also, in return for another seven years of work.' And Jacob did so.

He finished his week with Leah and then Laban gave him his daughter Rachel to be his wife. Laban gave his servant girl Bilhah to his daughter Rachel as her maidservant. Jacob lay with Rachel also and he loved Rachel more than Leah. And he worked for Laban another seven years.

## Bait and Switch

Isn't it amazing that sometimes even the trickster gets tricked? Jacob spent seven years working to marry Rachel but was deceived by Laban who was more cunning than he was. Caught in the mix of all of this were two women: Leah and Rachel. Rachel knew Jacob loved her, but her own father used her as a pawn to get seven years of free labor out of Jacob. You may have heard someone teach about poor old Leah and I agree that she was mistreated. But often people are inclined to assume that something is wrong with Rachel. You need to look at the situation from Rachel's perspective. She did not ask to be attractive, she was born that way. She did not ask Jacob to marry her, he fell in love with her. She certainly did not ask her father to trick him.

Rachel's situation is one of the classic examples of "don't hate me because I am beautiful." She had waited seven years for the man who loved her and now was put into a position of sharing what she thought was hers alone. She could even see the intensity of Jacob's love when he agreed to work another seven years for her after he had been tricked instead of leaving in anger. There is something very important you need to understand about Jacob's decision to pay an additional dowry for Rachel. He did not have to wait seven years to marry her as many have incorrectly concluded. Laban said he needed to finish his *bridal week* with Leah. In many eastern cultures, the bride was given a *bridal week* of her husband's undivided attention. After this Jacob marries Rachel and gave Laban another seven years of labor.

At this time in history, a woman's role in the household and family structure was very different than it is now. To be married and bear children, especially male children, was an expectation and considered a great honor. The wife was not expected to do much outside of the home responsibilities. Now these two sisters had been pitted against each other and only one of them was truly loved by their husband. The race was on to conceive and bear a male child who would be the principle heir of Jacob's household.

You may be able to identify with Rachel in this circumstance. You know exactly what you want to accomplish, you may even feel pressure to complete it quickly. When it does not happen in what you consider to be a reasonable amount of time, frustration can set in. Rachel faced an even more intense situation; in her mind she was in competition with her sister and things were not going her way.

> When the Lord saw that Leah was not loved, he
> opened her womb but Rachel was barren. Leah
> became pregnant and gave birth to a son. She
> named him Reuben, for she said, 'It is because he
> Lord has seen my misery. Surely my husband will
> love me now.' She conceived again, and when

she gave birth to a son she said, 'Because the Lord heard that I am not loved, he gave me this one too.' So she named Him Simeon. Again she conceived, and when she gave birth to a son she said, 'Now at last my husband will come attached to me, because I have borne him three sons.' So he was named Levi. She conceived again, and when she gave birth to a son she said, 'This time I will praise the Lord.' So she named him Judah. Then she stopped having children.

Genesis 29:31-35

## People Can Cause Delays

God saw that Leah was being mistreated so he enabled her to conceive early and often.  Jacob did not love her in the same way he loved Rachel yet she was the one who was bearing his children. It is interesting to note that Jacob did not even take an active role in naming his children. Rachel was forced to toil in frustration while her sister was able to accomplish the very same goal with ease.

In your personal experiences you may have seen your sisters in the faith appear to reach their goals and dreams while you seem to be going nowhere fast. You must learn not to be fooled by the outward appearance of circumstances, because often God is working behind the scenes. His timing is not always the same as yours, but it is always perfect. You may have been taught differently, but other people can delay your progress but they cannot keep you from reaching your ultimate goal. Rachel was not the cause of her delay; her husband Jacob was.

> When the Lord saw that Leah was not loved, he
> opened her womb, but Rachel was barren.
>
> Genesis 29:31

It was Jacob's mistreatment of Leah that caused the Lord to close Rachel's womb. He knew that Jacob needed to experience a change of heart. He was disciplining Jacob, not punishing Rachel. There may be occasions that God will hold back the manifestation of your vision because a key component that is beyond your control is not in place. God knows the right season to release the blessing into your life so that He may receive the maximum glory. He would not allow Rachel to have a son for Jacob before Leah because Jacob would be even more inclined to mistreat Leah. God's purpose required that Leah's children be born first. Rachel's firstborn would play a major role in the history of the nation of Israel, and his place in the birth order demanded that his arrival be delayed. Through the entire rivalry and surrogate pregnancies, God's divine plan was being manifested. The birth of Rachel's first child was a divine delay, and you may experience the same in your journey to fulfilling your vision. Just as in Rachel's situation, when the time comes, God's divine timing will move in your life.

> Then God remembered Rachel; he listened to
> her and opened her womb. She became
> pregnant and gave birth to a son and said, 'God
> has taken away my disgrace.' She named him
> Joseph, and said, 'May the Lord add to me
> another son.'
>
> Genesis 30:22-24

The birth of Joseph signaled a new season in the life of Rachel. This child was different from the ones who were conceived by her maidservant. Joseph was not the firstborn, but he was the favored son in the eyes of his father Jacob. He was also the son who carried the vision for the future of his people. His arrival was delayed in our human estimation, however in God's plan he was right on schedule.

You may be frustrated and ready to give up. You may feel that it is too late to accomplish the vision that God put in your heart. There is a strong possibility that you may be experiencing a divine delay. God may be testing your faithfulness while you are waiting on your prayer to be answered. He may want to open your eyes so that you can see your reaction when your sister gets the blessing before you. He is going to remove all doubt that He is in control of your life. He put the vision in your heart and He knows when it is time for it to manifest.

If you can remain obedient in your divine delay, just as Jacob adorned his son in a coat of many colors, God will have your vision stand out in the crowd and proclaim his favor upon you. He will let it be known that you are highly favored. You need to pray for patience and strength to persevere in your divine delay. Move a step beyond Rachel and learn to celebrate when your sisters conceive and give birth to their vision. Their success should be a reminder that God is faithful to His word.

Do not be deceived by the spiritual forces that will attack your mind into thinking that others did not have to struggle as you did. They have just come into their season and soon it will be your turn. The private struggles you endured while remaining faithful will not be in vain. For what you have done in secret the Lord will reward you openly. Jacob had to work for years to have Rachel as his wife so that she could conceive and give birth. Remember that Jesus gave His life that you might be able to conceive and give birth to your vision. As Solomon has said:

> There is a time for everything, and a season for every activity under heaven.
>
> Ecclesiastes 3:1

Your season is on its way.

# Part III

# LABOR

## CHAPTER SIX
# Get Ready For a Breakthrough

MOST OF US start off pursuing our goals with a high level of expectation. As we experience the ups and downs of the journey, our emotions can begin to take a more prominent role in our thought patterns. When you can see a light at the end of the tunnel you may experience a burst of energy, but when the road looks dark you may have the tendency to become discouraged. The key to each situation is your expectation. Whether positive or negative, your level of expectation will increase in the corresponding direction that you see your circumstance. If you are going to be one of the few that walk by faith and pursue your vision, you must develop a steadfast ability to remain constant regardless of what is going on around you to experience a breakthrough in your destiny. The people, places, and situations in your life can change at a moment's notice, but the promises of God are always true.

In Genesis Chapter 38 we find a woman who was put into a situation that she had little or no control over. Judah, the son of Jacob, went to live in the Canaanite town of Adullam. There he met and married a Canaanite woman named Shua who gave birth to three sons Er, Onan, and Shelah. After a few years Judah found a wife for his son Er.

> Judah got a wife for Er, his firstborn, and her name was Tamar. But Er, Judah's firstborn, was wicked in the Lord's sight; so the Lord put him to death.
>
> Genesis 38:6-7

Tamar was a Canaanite woman who married a man who was wicked in the sight of God. Her only responsibility was to bear children in her husband's name, but she was denied that opportunity because of her husband's sin. God put him to death and she was left childless. In the custom of that time the next eldest brother was responsible for raising children in his brother's name.

> Then Judah said to Onan, 'Lie with your brother's wife and fulfill your duty as her brother-in-law to produce offspring for your brother.'
>
> Genesis 38:8

It would seem that Tamar had a reason to expect that she would not be left childless and dishonored. She willingly accepted the tradition of that day knowing any children that were conceived would receive the inheritance of her late husband.

> But Onan knew that the offspring would not be his; so whenever he laid with his brother's wife, he spilled his semen on the ground to keep from producing offspring for his brother. What he did was wicked in the Lord's sight; so he put him to death also.
>
> Genesis 38:9-10

Tamar gave herself willingly, but because she was involved with a selfish man she received nothing in return. He withheld the one thing she needed but could not produce on her own just to protect his own interest. So Tamar for a second time was left alone and barren after living with expectation. It seemed as if her breakthrough was going to elude her. Perhaps you have trusted or relied on people to give you something that does not cost them anything, but would be a great blessing to you, yet they withhold it because of selfishness or insecurity. You may have been on a job where your superiors refused to train you; therefore you could not be promoted. Perhaps a friend refused to share financial advice that could get you out of debt. No matter what the situation, the frustration is still the same. Someone or something is causing your breakthrough to be withheld. In Tamar's situation, God put both men to death and although she was no longer being mistreated, she was still unfulfilled, and about to feel the effects of another selfish man.

> Judah then said to his daughter-in-law Tamar, 'Live as a widow in your father's house until my son Shelah grows up.' For he thought he may die too, just like his brothers. So Tamar went to live in her father's house.
>
> Genesis 38:11

Tamar was once again obedient not knowing she was the victim of a selfish man's fear. Although Judah feared for his son's life, it appears he made little or no attempt to teach him to live a life that is pleasing to God. Tamar spent years in her father's house waiting for the time when she would have the opportunity to fulfill her destiny. She could see a light at the end of the tunnel, but she would soon discover it was only a reflection of the selfishness of her father-in-law. In her frustration she too was about to make a critical error.

> After a long time Judah's wife, the daughter of Shua, died. When Judah recovered from his grief, he went to Timnah, to the men who were shearing his sheep, and his friend Hirah the Adullamite went with him. When Tamar was told 'Your father-in –law is on his way to Timnah, to sheer his sheep,' she took off her widow's clothes, covered herself with a veil to disguise herself, and sat down at the entrance of Enaim which is on the road to Timnah. For she saw that, though Shelah had now grown up she had not been given to him as his wife.
>
> Genesis 38:12-14

## Never Compromise Integrity In Pursuit of Your Vision

Tamar knew Judah had duped her because when the time came she was not allowed to marry Shelah. She then made the mistake of allowing her frustration to boil over into an act of deception. Even after she had been mistreated, she should have learned from the men who had been in her life that God will judge those who do wrong. But seeing her father-in-law carrying on with business as usual was too much for her to bear. She was determined to have what she desired, even if it meant using trickery to get it. Blinded by her frustration, she was willing to belittle herself to take away the shame of being barren. She also had a secondary motive. Because she had no husband, she had no real means of support. Just as in today society, many women lower their standards and live in degrading situations for economic security. God never intended for a woman to submit her body or her mind to a man who did not have her best interests at heart. But in the heat of the moment many women just like Tamar make that fatal decision.

> When Judah saw her he thought she was a (temple) prostitute, for she had covered her face. Not realizing she was his daughter-in-law, he went over to her by the roadside and said, 'Come now let me sleep with you. And what will you give me to sleep with you?' she asked. 'I'll send you a young goat from my flock' he said. 'Will you give me something as a pledge until you send it?' she asked. He said, 'What shall I give you? Your cord and the staff in your hand' she answered. So he gave them to her and he slept with her and she became pregnant by him.
>
> Genesis 38:15-18

Judah believed he was sleeping with a temple prostitute so he thought nothing of his sinful act. However, when he sent payment in the form of a goat he was shocked and embarrassed to find out she was nowhere to be found. Tamar's situation was not on his mind because he was more concerned about his reputation. He had the power to restore her name by giving her his son Shelah as her husband so that she could bear a child. Yet, he refused. He did not know that she now had his reputation in her hands.

> About three months later Judah was told, 'Your
> daughter-in-law is guilty of prostitution, and as a
> result she is now pregnant.' Judah said, 'Bring her
> out and have her burned to death!' as she was
> being brought out, she sent a message to her
> father-in-law. 'I am pregnant by the man who
> owns these.' She said. And she added, 'See if you
> recognize whose seal and cord and staff these are.'
> Judah recognized them and said, 'She is more
> righteous than I since I wouldn't give her to my
> son Shelah.' And he did not sleep with her again.
>
> Genesis 38:24-26

When you look at Tamar and what she did in attempting
to redeem her honor, you may be inclined to believe she was
in some way justified in her actions. Judah's statement "She
is more righteous than I" may hold some truth to it but God
was not pleased with Tamar's behavior. Tamar's story
should be a lesson in allowing God to vindicate you when
you have been mistreated. She was pregnant but would
never be able to marry Shelah or any other man, which was
a very heavy price to pay. Judah was ready to have her
burned alive not knowing she was carrying his offspring.
However, God is able to take even your worst mistakes and
use them for your good and His glory. Even in the midst of
your greatest error, God is able to give you a breakthrough.

> When the time came for her to give birth, there
> were twin boys in her womb. She was giving
> birth, one of them put out his hand; so the
> midwife took a scarlet thread and tied it on his
> wrist and said 'This one came first.' But when he

drew back his hand, his brother came out, and
she said, 'So this is how you have broken out!'
And his name was Perez.

Genesis 38:27-29

Tamar's son Perez, which means *breakthrough*, was
conceived by deception but was used to deliver Tamar from
her shame. God took Judah's sinful act and Tamar's trickery
and molded a child that would be in the family line of Jesus
(Matthew1: 3), and He is able to do the same for you.
Never purposely do things that are wrong and try to justify
them. However you should not underestimate God's ability
to use your shortcomings for His good. God's grace is much
bigger than any sin you may have committed. He is ready to
give you a breakthrough just as He has done in times past.

Samson took God's anointing of strength for granted,
but even in death he was able to crush his enemy. David had
his friend Uriah murdered to cover up his sin with
Bathsheba, which resulted in the death of the child they
conceived. However, God later blessed them with Solomon,
the wisest king in Israel's history. Peter denied that he knew
Jesus when Jesus could have used his support the most; yet
he was not only restored, but became one of the greatest
leaders the church has ever known. None of these
individuals were justified in their actions but God gave them
a breakthrough anyway.

Don't let your past ruin your future or allow a feeling of
inadequacy rob you of the provision God has for you. Be
encouraged by the events of Tamar's delivery and let the
scarlet thread that was tied around the wrist of the second
son remind you that the blood of Christ has come out

before you and cleansed you. God has a *Perez*, a breakthrough, prepared for you. There is a light that is at the end of the tunnel that cannot be extinguished. Commit yourself to your God-inspired vision and get ready for your breakthrough.

# CHAPTER SEVEN
# The Restoration Power
# of Conception

MANY OF US have had the unfortunate experience of turning on our computer only to find out that it has been infected with a virus. You are acutely aware that anything that has not been saved on a separate device is in danger of being erased. My wife and I became victims of this problem, and by the time the virus was eliminated we had lost everything except the original programs of the computer. We had to go through the process of reinstalling several programs, and some things could not be recovered and were lost forever. We did not have to replace any parts on the computer, but we did have to hire someone to get them to function properly. It is the same principle you may use when having your car serviced. You turn the key and it will not start. You may not even bother to lift the hood if you don't know anything about cars. You get the vehicle to your mechanic and hopefully with the help of his tools, your vehicle will be running within a few hours without any parts being replaced, only repaired.

The similarity between the computer and the car is that when you use these items, you expect them to work properly. In fact, you are often shocked when they do not. Your life can function the same way. You know you have all of the parts to help complete your assignment, but they sometimes do not function in the way that would allow you to achieve success.

In the thirteenth chapter of the book of Judges we find a story of a woman whose name is not mentioned but her story is common. She was the wife of a man named Monoah from the tribe of Dan. She was suffering in her body in a way that you may be suffering in relationship to your destiny.

> Again the Israelites did evil in the eyes of the Lord, so he delivered them into the hands of the Philistines for forty years. A certain man of Zorah, named Manoah, from the clan of the Danites, had a wife who was sterile and remained childless. The angel of the Lord appeared to her and said, 'You are sterile and childless, but you are going to conceive and have a son. Now see to it that you drink no wine or fermented drink and that you do not eat anything unclean, because you will conceive and give birth to son. No razor may be used upon his head, because the boy is to be a Nazirite, set apart to God from birth, and he will begin the deliverance of Israel from the hands of the Philistines.'
>
> Judges 13:1-5

## Damaged Wombs Can't Conceive

Manoah's wife (I will call her Mona to keep from being so impersonal) had an encounter that would change her whole outlook on her future. She was a woman who had all the parts that were necessary to conceive, yet they were not functioning properly. The Hebrew word *aqar* used in this passage to describe her condition of being barren was put into a different *stem* to indicate that she had some sort of physical malady that prevented her from conceiving. The angel of the Lord pointed this out by saying she was sterile and childless, but that was about to change. Mona believed what the angel of the Lord had said and went to her husband to tell him the good news. She emphasized that the child was to be a Nazirite all of his life. The Nazirite vow is found in the book of Numbers chapter six. These were men who were set apart for special service to the Lord. The vow could be for a specified time or for life. This was a covenant agreement between the individual and God. Mona's son was to be a deliverer. He was called to begin the process of liberating Israel from the Philistines.

## Get Proper Instruction from the Lord

God was going to restore Mona's womb to help restore his people. God was the one who initiated the Nazirite covenant, however it was still Mona's responsibility to adhere to it. A covenant is an agreement between two or more parties. God always keeps his part of the agreement, and when we keep ours the desired result is guaranteed. When she told her husband what had happened, he was quick to ask for help from God to make sure he would be able to properly care for the child.

> Then Manoah prayed to the Lord: 'O Lord I beg
> you, let the man of God you sent to us come

again to teach how to bring up the boy who is to
be born. God heard Manoah, and the angel of
God came again to the woman while she was out
in the field; but her husband was not with her.
The woman hurried to tell her husband, 'He is
here the man who appeared to me the other day!
Manoah got up and followed his wife. When he
came to the man, he said, 'Are you the one who
talked to my wife? 'I am' he said. So Manoah ask
him ask him, 'When your words are fulfilled,
what is to be the rule for the boy's life and work?

Judges 13:8-12

## Honor the Covenant

The Angel of the Lord repeated the words he had spoken to
Manoah's wife. He said that she would need to adhere to
the Nazirite covenant and raise her son under that covenant
his entire life. God was initiating this agreement because he
was going to begin the deliverance of Israel from the
Philistines. God was going to demonstrate the power of
restoration through covenant. You may be wondering how
any of this relates to your destiny. You must understand that
the Bible is a book of covenants and many of the promises
of God are based on His covenant relationship with His
children. He wants to restore the damaged places in your
life so that you can fulfill your destiny. His covenants are
designed to keep you from sabotaging your potential and in
many instances to draw you closer to Him. Manoah's wife
was born to carry the seed that God was going to use to
bless Israel. Although she was not going to be a Nazirite, she

had to keep the covenant to protect the seed. In your life you must learn to keep the covenants that God has set forth for you to protect the seed of destiny He has planted in you.

When we draw from some principles found in the Nazirite vow, it becomes clear that a covenant relationship with God is the key to restoring and maintaining the promise. The first vow was not to drink any fermented drink or anything that comes from a grapevine. One of the things that grape juice can produce is wine. With wine you have the potential to become intoxicated and do things you would not do in a sober state. In the same manner you would do well not to expose your mind to the intoxicating temptations of this world. There are many things that appear to be harmless in moderation, but in actuality they pose a deadly threat. A pregnant woman may not be harmed by alcohol, but her baby is at risk by even a small amount. The vision for your life is also vulnerable to things that may seem to have no visible effect on you. When God begins the process of restoring your womb after it has been damaged, do not allow yourself to do things to hinder the restoration.

Mona was also instructed not to eat anything unclean. The Laws given by Moses to the people of Israel on what foods were considered clean were very clear. They were designed to keep the people healthy and also to serve as a sign of the covenant with God. In the same way you need to make sure the food that you are feeding your soul is clean. You cannot expect God to complete a work of restoration in your life while you consume the garbage of the world. If you have close relationships with people who are feeding garbage into your soul, get away from them. You need to keep the work of restoration in your life pure so that the *rhema* word you receive from God does not have to be filtered through trash you have allowed to rest in your soul.

A Nazirite vow also demanded that the one who accepted the vow keep away from things that were dead. You need to understand that nothing really has life unless it is connected to God. That is why the scripture says he who has the *Son* has life and he who does not have the Son does not have life (1 John 5:12). But one of the dangers of coming into contact with things that are dead is that they have the ability to spread disease and cause other things to die. A dead animal left out in the open will be full of bacteria in just a few hours. These tiny organisms serve a purpose for the dead but not for the living. If you come into contact with them they have the ability to kill you. From a spiritual perspective you must stay away from dream killers, no matter how insignificant they may appear to be.

Finally there was the command that the child's hair should never be cut. This was an outward and obvious sign that the child was in covenant with God. The danger of a gift that is visible to all is that you may be tempted to exploit it. If you read the story of Samson, the child who was conceived, you will find that his gifts of great strength were well known by his enemies, but the secret of his covenant was not. When he began to abuse it and take his power for granted, he allowed himself to be deceived. The result was that the enemy found the source of his strength and cut it off. The power was not his hair but the covenant his hair represented. If you read the complete story, you learn that he was able to have his strength restored for one final attack on the enemy after his hair grew back—but he had to come to God and request the covenant be restored.

Do not take the things God has restored in your life for granted. Do not expose them to people or things that tear them down instead of build them up. God is ready to do a work of restoration in your life so that you can conceive your dream, but it is up to you to protect and respect what He has provided. If you are ready to do those things you are ready to acquire the keys that will assist you in giving birth to the vision of your heart.

Part IV

# DELIVERY

# CHAPTER EIGHT
# Redemption: the Master Plan
# of Conception

IMAGINE YOURSELF holding a garage sale to get rid of some junk you have been storing in your attic for years. Strangers come by and browse through the items hoping to find some knick-knack to accent their home. A woman finds an old tarnished letter opener and makes what you feel to be a generous offer. You accept and feel good about the transaction until a sickening sensation hits your stomach. You realize that, by mistake, you have just sold a family heirloom passed down through the generations. You move with haste and stop the woman before she drives off. She is surprised to hear you offer twice what she just paid for it to get it back. When she is hesitant to sell it back, you offer her three times what she paid and she reluctantly agrees. She did not realize you would have paid ten times as much if necessary to get that letter opener back. After the sale you take the opener inside and apply some tarnish remover and the true beauty of the item is revealed. That is a demonstration of the passion that is behind the power of redemption: to be willing to buy back something that you once owned because you know its hidden value. You may have given away or sold your dream below its value, and you must be willing to pay the cost to get it back into your possession.

In the book of Ruth we find a man named Elimelech, his wife Naomi and their two sons Mahlon and Killian living in Bethlehem. When the crops failed and famine begins to ravage the land they move to Moab, where, after Elimelech's death, his sons marry Moabite women named Orpah and Ruth. Later both of the sons die leaving behind two widows and a mother with no one to care for them. When Naomi heard that that Lord had come to the aid of his people in Judah, she decided to return back to Judah.

> Then Naomi said to her two daughters in law, 'Go back, each of you to your mother's home. May the Lord show kindness to both of you, as you have to your dead and me. May the Lord grant that each of you find rest in the home of another husband.' Then she kissed them and they wept aloud.
>
> Ruth 1:8-9

Naomi knew the future did not look bright for her daughters-in-law in Bethlehem of Judah. Not only were they foreigners, but their family's ancestors were despised by the Jewish people; they were Moabite women, descendants of a race of people who were the result of the incest of Lot and his daughters. In addition, Moabites were enemies of Israel because their king had tried to pay a prophet to speak curses on the people. According to the Law of Moses, they were not allowed to enter into the assembly of the people of God for ten generations, or even sign a peace treaty with them (Deuteronomy 23:3-6). At Naomi's insistence Orpah remained in Moab, but Ruth made a critical life changing decision.

But Ruth replied, 'don't urge me to leave or turn back from you. Where you go I will go and where you stay I will stay. Your people will be my people and your God my God. Where you die I will die and there I will be buried. May the Lord deal with me be it ever so severely, if anything but death separates you and me.'

Ruth 1:16-17

Naomi realized Ruth was not going to give up so she stopped trying to keep her from coming. Ruth was a barren widow headed for a country where her people were despised, but she had decided to turn from the false gods of that land and serve the true and living God. She went with her mother knowing they had no means to support themselves. However, she was convinced that even as an outcast she had more to gain going with Naomi than staying where she was.

## Your Dream Does Not Come With a Coupon

You will have times in your life when you must assess the pros and cons of a critical decision. Where you place your value will play a pivotal role in helping you choose the correct path to take. You may also face a time when the best decision may cost you everything you have and you may not be guaranteed to get it back. Your destiny should determine your decisions and your mind should be focused on how things will be affected in the long run. In order to do that you must have a master plan of what you truly desire to achieve. As a business student, one of the very first things I learned is that every successful company has a mission statement. It is an official decree of why the company exists and what they intend to do. Just as Ruth was determined to remain with Naomi and the people of God at any cost, you must be willing to pay any price to acquire or redeem your vision. You must have a master plan for your life that you are willing to follow at all costs and will not compromise.

After arriving in Bethlehem, Ruth lived with her mother-in-law and went out into the field to pick up some loose grain on the edge of the field as foreigners were allowed to do according to the law (Leviticus 19: 9-10). What she did not know was the field she had chosen belonged to Boaz, a relative of her deceased husband. When he saw her gathering wheat in the field he approached her and praised her for the kindness she had shown to Naomi. He invited her to a meal and instructed his workers to leave extra grain in her path to make sure she had more than enough. He even offered to let her stay with his servant girls during the harvest. This was an amazing act of God considering Ruth's situation. She was a foreigner from an idolatrous people; yet God had opened up a door of opportunity because of her faithfulness. This should encourage you because you can be assured that while you are giving birth to the vision of your heart, your faithfulness to God will not go unrewarded. God's master plan is at work in your life and you will always receive more than what you give when you align your vision with His purposes.

## Recognizing Your Redeemer

Naomi was elated to find out that Boaz had shown kindness to Ruth and that he was concerned about the welfare of his relatives. She encouraged Ruth to remain with the servant

girls until the harvest was over. She desired to find someone
to take care of Ruth, and Boaz seemed perfect for the job.

> Wash and perfume yourself and put on your best
> clothes, then go down to the threshing floor, but
> do not let him know you are there until he has
> finished eating and drinking. When he lays down
> note the place where he is lying. Then uncover
> his feet and lie down. He will know what to do.
>
> Ruth 3:3-4

Naomi sent Ruth to initiate a process with Boaz that
would change all of their lives forever. When Boaz was
awakened by something in the middle of the night he saw a
woman lying at his feet.

> 'Who are you?' he asked 'I am Ruth' she said
> 'Spread the corner of your garment over me,
> since you are a kinsman redeemer.'
>
> Ruth 3:9

Naomi knew something Ruth did not, the law of the
kinsman redeemer. She literally sent Ruth to Boaz to offer
herself in marriage. He, as a relative had the right to raise
children in the name of her deceased husband. That would
be the only way to maintain the family property because it
must be passed down to a male heir. Boaz was surprised she
chose him instead of pursuing a younger man. He was
willing to forfeit the inheritance of property, but he was
compelled to follow the procedure for a redeeming relative
found in the law in Leviticus 25, which states the closest
relative had first opportunity to redeem the property
owned. He sent Ruth home to Naomi and called a meeting

of the elders at the city gate. When presented with the opportunity, the relative who was first in line to redeem the property Naomi was selling accepted. Boaz then informed him of the responsibility that came along with it.

> Then Boaz said 'On the day you buy the land from Naomi and from Ruth the Moabite you acquire the dead man's widow in order to maintain the dead with his property.' At this the kinsman redeemer said, 'I cannot redeem it because it may endanger my own estate. You redeem it yourself. I cannot do it."
>
> Ruth 4:5-6

## You Are Worth the Price Paid For You

The redeemer who was first in line could afford to pay the price but was not willing to make the commitment. Boaz was willing to pay and take on the responsibility as the redeemer even if it meant maintaining the legacy of Ruth's previous husband instead of his own. In light of that, understand that God looked at you in your state of sin and despair and decided that you were worth the price he had to pay. God saw a value in you that that he was willing to give of Himself in order to set you free.

> For this reason Christ is the mediator of a new covenant that those who are called may receive the promised eternal inheritance — now that he has died as a ransom (redemption) to set them free from the sins committed under the first covenant.
>
> Hebrews 9:15

This act of love was not only for you to receive eternal life. God placed gifts and abilities in you that he needed to salvage before they were lost.

> For we are God's workmanship, created in Christ Jesus to do good works, which God prepared in advance for us to do.
>
> Ephesians 2:10

God did not redeem you just so you could stay where you are but to do good works He had prepared for you before you were in your mother's womb. Why is this? Because God has a master plan, a primary mission in which the central focus is that all of his creation receive eternal life and enter into his kingdom. Therefore, any vision that He plants in you must at its core be designed to assist God in accomplishing His master plan.

Your vision is connected to God's master plan of redemption for all mankind. Before you had a relationship with him through Jesus Christ, you were an outsider like Ruth but God knew the vision He planted in you and paid the price of redemption to give you an opportunity to fulfill it. All of us were born outside of fellowship with God. It was the sacrifice of Jesus that allowed us to come into right relationship with Him. Jesus is your Kinsman Redeemer and He initiated the Father's master plan with His death, burial, and resurrection. He paid the price for all so that any who receive His gift may in like manner help fulfill the master plan of the Father.

> But do not forget this one thing, dear friends: With the Lord a day is like a thousand years, and

a thousand years like a day. The Lord is not slow
in keeping His promise, as some understand
slowness. He is patient with you, not wanting
any to perish, but everyone to come to
repentance.

2 Peter 3:8-9

No matter what your vision is it should be in line with
the master plan of God. It should lead people to God and
not away from Him. You may have to face many obstacles
and difficulties as Ruth did, but you must also develop a
master plan for your life. God's Kinsman Redeemer for
man, Jesus Christ, paid the price for a mighty conception to
take place and be given life through you. Ruth came from a
people that were conceived in wickedness, steeped in
idolatry, and enemies of the chosen people of God. She had
not proven herself capable of producing offspring and she
was outside of proper covenant with God, yet He saw fit to
redeem her. Why did He do it? He did it because out of
Ruth would come Obed, and from Obed would come Jesse,
and from Jesse would come David and through the
generations leading up to the birth of Jesus. Line up with
God's master plan and prepare yourself to give birth to the
greatness in you.

# CHAPTER NINE
# Worship: the Master Key to Conception

YOUR RESPONSE to a request for assistance may be in direct correlation of how you are approached. A husband who politely ask his wife to prepare his favorite meal is very likely to receive it. If he shouts and demands that it be prepared immediately, he may still get it, *but might be afraid to eat it*. When petitioning God you need to be aware that His response may also depend on the manner in which He is approached and the spirit in which the request is made.

> God opposes the proud but gives grace to the humble.
>
> 1 Peter 5:5

You must remember that even your right to approach God for your needs and desires was paid for by someone else. You should have confidence that you will receive your request, not because of your good deeds, but because of His grace. It is by relationship that we approach God with our request. You probably would not think of asking a stranger to lend you their car. It would seem almost unimaginable to show up at the White House unannounced and expect to have lunch with the president. It is not that the president is above you, it is that you do not have that type of relationship with him.

## God's Desire Is to Be Worshipped

God is self-sufficient; however, he does desire to be worshipped. Worshipping God is different from praising Him. We praise God for what He has done. Everyone can do that because God provides many blessings without being asked. Even people who do not have a proper relationship with God will praise Him for the blessings they receive. However, in order to worship God you must know who He is. Worship involves intimacy. Worshipping God because He is all you need and desire is what God is looking for. He desires true worship from someone who will say, "Before I ask I will acknowledge your greatness. Before I request I will sing of your loving and kind nature. I will not approach you with an open hand but with uplifted hands."

There was a woman in Samaria who had a very poor concept of worship. An encounter with Jesus would change her life forever. By a well where Jesus was sitting, she was drawing water in the middle of the day. This was not the best time for such work because of the heat and the amount of effort it took to draw the water. It is possible she may have been drawing water at this time of day to escape the scorn and ridicule of those who knew her history. Jesus asked her for a drink of water knowing how she would react because Jews and Samaritans did not associate with each other. The way she addressed Jesus during their encounter sheds a bright light on how our relationship with God determines our ability to worship.

The Samaritan woman said to him, "**You** are a Jew and I am a Samaritan. How can you ask me for a drink?"(For Jews did not associate with Samaritans.) Jesus answered her 'If you knew the gift of God and whom it is that ask you for a drink you would have asked him and he would have given you living water'. '**Sir** you have nothing to draw with and the well is too deep. Where can you get this living water? Are you greater than our father Jacob, who gave us this well and drank from it himself, as did his sons and his flocks and herds?'

John 4:9-12

## Your Perception of God Affects Your Worship

Her original reaction was of disdain because she knew Jews and Samaritans would not even drink from the same cup. But the power and presence of the Spirit of God had already begun to change the way she saw Jesus. She had changed her response from *You* to *Sir*.

Jesus answered, 'Everyone who drinks this water will be thirsty again, but whoever drinks the water I give him will never thirst. Indeed the water I give him will become in him a spring of water welling up to eternal life.' The woman said to him '**Sir** give me this water so that so that I won't get thirsty and have to keep coming here to draw water.'

John 4:13-15

Originally she was attempting to verify her relationship with God because of her heritage as a descendent of the sons of Jacob. She believed the Samaritans who worship on that mountain instead of in the Jewish temple were superior. After hearing Jesus' words she preferred to have the living water Jesus spoke of, which would keep her from facing ridicule.

> He told her, 'Go call your husband and come back. 'I have no husband', she replied. Jesus said to her, 'You are right to say when you say you have no husband. The fact is you have had five husbands and the man you now have is not your husband. What you have just said is quite true.' 'Sir', the woman said 'I can see you are a **prophet.** Our father worshipped on this mountain, but you Jews claim we must worship in Jerusalem.'
>
> John 4:16-19

It is amazing that in a brief encounter her perspective of Jesus changed from **You** to **Sir** to **Prophet.** She was still focused on where and not how to approach God. She knew in her heart the words that Jesus spoke to her were true, but her views still had residue from the way she was raised to believe what the proper way was to worship God.

> Jesus declared, 'Believe me woman a time is coming when you will worship the Father neither on this mountain, nor in Jerusalem. You Samaritans worship what you do not know; We worship what we do know, for salvation is of the

Jews. Yet a time is coming and has now come when the true worshippers will worship the father in spirit and in truth, for they are the kind of worshippers the Father seeks. God is spirit, and his worshippers must worship in spirit and in truth.'

John 4:21-24

The woman at the well was waiting for the one who would come and reveal these truths to her. She told Jesus she believed the Messiah would one day come and explain how to obtain the intimate relationship with God she longed for. When Jesus declared He was the one she was seeking she left her water pot, forgot the opinions the people had about her and ran into town saying:

'Come see a man who told me everything I ever did. Could this be the **Christ**?

John 4:29

Jesus told her the Father was seeking true worshippers. The living water He spoke of is the Holy Spirit, and He would spring up eternally. You must understand that it is by covenant relationship through Jesus Christ that you approach God and by spirit that you worship Him. It is worship that draws you closer to God. A person who is a worshipper proves that although they come to God with their petitions, they are more interested in His presence that in receiving His presents.

Having a lifestyle of worship regardless of your circumstance is a decision you must make before pursuing your dream in life. There will be times when life just seems unfair and you in your natural mind may question the value of continuing to serve God while your troubles seem to persist. Add to that the reality that people who do not look at worship as a priority seem to prosper effortlessly and you may be tempted to breakdown and give up.

In the book of First Samuel we find a man named Elkanah who had two wives Hannah and Peninnah. Peninnah had children but Hannah was barren and going to the house of worship was taking a toll on her.

> Year after year this man went up from his town to worship and sacrifice to the Lord Almighty at Shiloh, where Hophni and Phinehas, the two sons of Eli, were priest of the Lord. Whenever the day came for Elkanah to sacrifice he would give portions of the meat to his wife Peninnah and to all her sons and daughters. But to Hannah he gave a double portion because he loved her, and the Lord had closed her womb.
>
> 1 Samuel 1:3-5

This was a thoughtful gesture on behalf of Elkanah; many men during this time in history would have divorced a barren wife. He showed her affection by giving her twice as much as Peninnah. Surely Hannah was appreciative of her husband but his kindness could not dull the pain of her barren womb. The one thing she desired, a child, was a constant source of frustration. So much so that even during times of worship she was disheartened. At the same time she had to endure the sight and sound of Peninnah and her children. You may have at times in your life experienced a similar frustration. The good thing that you are trying to do comes so easily to others yet so difficultly for you. In addition to all of Hannah's troubles, Peninnah mocked her constantly, most likely because she was jealous of Elkanah's affection for Hannah.

> And because the Lord had closed up her womb, her rival kept provoking her in order to irritate her. This went on year after year. Whenever Hannah would go up to the house of the Lord her rival provoked her till she wept and would not eat.
>
> 1 Samuel 1:6-7

If you notice, her rival would provoke her to tears when they went to the house of God to sacrifice and worship. The enemies of your dream whether they are spiritual or natural will try to steal your joy and provoke you in the same manner. The most hurtful persecution you receive while conceiving your dream and giving birth to your vision may not be from outside the church but from within. Hannah would become so upset she would not even be able to eat. She was going to the house of God just like you do, sacrificing just like you, and broken in spirit just like you may be at this very moment. Her inability to produce a child was a public humiliation and a private heartbreak. Even if you are in a situation where you are being persecuted in pursuit of your dream remember:

> No weapon forged against you will prevail and you will refute every tongue that accuses you. This is the heritage of the servants of the Lord, and this is their vindication from me declares the Lord.
>
> Isaiah 54:17

## Sugar Doesn't Always Make It Taste Better

There will also be times when those who mean well will do more harm than good. Elkanah saw his wife's misery and tried to comfort her, but his words only caused more heartache.

> Elkanah her husband would say to her, 'Hannah why are you weeping? Why don't you eat? Why are you downhearted? Don't I mean more to you than ten sons?'
>
> 1Samuel 1:8

His questions were sincere and his motives pure, but his insensitivity to Hannah's need for real fulfillment was obvious. Her need had nothing to do with him, but it was entrenched in how Hannah felt about herself. There will be times on the journey of giving birth to your vision that you may encounter individuals who cannot comprehend how you could possibly be unhappy with things that they would gladly settle for. Fortunately, Peninnahs' taunting, Elkanah's unintentional insensitivity and Hannah's longing for fulfillment led her back to the only one who could help her. She became so frustrated she went back into the temple to pray.

> In bitterness of soul Hannah wept much and prayed to the Lord. And she made a vow saying, 'O Lord Almighty, if you will look upon your servant's misery and remember me, and not forget your servant, but give her a son, then I will give him to the Lord for all the days of his life and razor will never be used on his head.'
>
> 1 Samuel 1:10-11

Hannah initiated a covenant with God that if he would give her a son she would dedicate him a Nazirite and for lifelong service to the Lord. As a believer you have the right to exercise your covenant relationship with God through Jesus Christ. But remember to keep your promise because God always keeps His, and He expects you to do the same. When God does something great for you, acknowledge Him and be sure to let others know that it was not solely in your own might, but by God's grace that you have been blessed.

## True Worship Is Peculiar To Most People

Everyone will not understand the way you approach God with your needs. When Eli the priest saw Hannah praying, he thought she was drunk and scolded her. When he realized she was praying through her pain he blessed her. This hurting soul had endured an unwarranted reprimand from the preacher, but her decision to pray opened up her eyes to the master key that would bring true fulfillment to her life after years of frustration. In times past, she would be so bitter in spirit she would not eat or even go to church. Does this sound familiar to you? When on a Sunday morning in a troubled season of your life, instead of going to the house of worship for healing you bury your head down and wallow in misery at Bedside Baptist. Never let your frustrations take you away from God, but use them to draw you closer to Him.

> Eli answered, 'Go in peace, and may the God of Israel grant you what you have asked of him.' She said, 'May your servant find favor in your

> eyes.' Then she went away and ate something
> and her face was no longer downcast.
>
> 1 Samuel 1:17-18

Hannah's actions after prayer indicate she expected God to do something on her behalf. **Prayer** and **faith** are essential elements in giving birth to your vision. However there is one more step you must take.

> Early the next morning they arose and
> **worshipped** before the Lord and went back to
> their home in Ramah. Elkanah lay with his wife
> and the Lord remembered her. So in the course
> of time Hannah conceived and gave birth to a
> son. She named him Samuel, saying 'Because I
> asked the Lord for Him.'
>
> 1 Samuel 1:19-20

In the same temple that she suffered harassment, the same place Hannah became so bitter in spirit she could not eat and still with a barren womb, Hannah *worshipped* God. This was the master key that unlocked God's favor upon her. She conceived and gave birth to the son she had petitioned God for, and true to her word, she dedicated him to the service of the Lord at the temple as promised.

What a great story. A woman bitter in spirit worships God and is rewarded. But it does not end there. Hannah, after dedicating Samuel at the Temple, later gives birth to three more sons and two daughters (1 Samuel 2:21). If you develop a lifestyle of worship, God will do the same for you.

Now to him who is able to do immeasurably more than we ask or imagine according to the power that is at work in us.

Ephesians 3:20

God's love is so great that he will do more than what you ask of Him. As a believer you have an advantage that Hannah did not. You have the Spirit of God dwelling inside of you. Worship God before and after you conceive and unlock the floodgate of blessing God has prepared for your vision.

# CHAPTER TEN
# Love: the Master Motivator of Conception

IN TODAY'S SOCIETY the idea of real love is tossed around like a play toy. People confuse love with infatuation and even lust. You need to be aware that God takes the idea of true love seriously. The English language is very limited at times in its ability to express the way that love is being emphasized to its beneficiary. The word of God has a great deal to say about love, and you would be wise to seek out its revelatory truths. When you understand love from a biblical standpoint, you gain insight into God's nature and why he created man. You will also see why love is such an important part of fulfilling your vision.

> For he chose us in Him before the creation of the world, to be holy and blameless in his sight. In love he predestined us adopted as his sons through Jesus Christ in accordance to his pleasure and good will.
>
> Ephesians 1:4-5

You can see from the word, that God chose us before the world was created and predestined us, in love, to be his sons through Jesus Christ. Part of God's plan was to have sons to fellowship with. I believe God did this because it is a reflection of His nature. John writes:

> Dear friends, let us love one another, for love comes from God. Everyone who loves has been born of God and knows God. Whoever does not love does not know God, because God is love.
>
> 1 John 4:7-8

## Pure Love Is Found In God

John is saying in order to know God, you must have love. The Greek word used in this passage for the word *know*, is *ginosko*, which implies having a relationship that is beyond casual. I like to use the definition of love I learned from Dr. Ed Cole. He describes love as **the desire to give at the expense of self to benefit others.** True love involves giving and that is an integral part of the nature of God. How can we know this? The Greek language gives us the deeper meanings for love and uses several different words to bring out its nuances. When we read:

> For God so loved the world that he gave his one and only Son, that whoever believes in him will not perish but have eternal life.
>
> John 3:16

We can see that the word for love used is the Greek word *agape*. This is the kind of love that does not require reciprocation. God gave his only begotten Son so we could have eternal life and fellowship with Him. He had to give His Son because true love involves giving and we know that

He chose us in Himself. Why did he do this? Because *God is love.*

In the book of 2 Kings we find the story of a woman who was full of love for God but barren in her womb.

> One day Elisha went to Shunem. And a well to do woman was there who urged him to stay for a meal. So whenever he came by, he stopped to eat there. She said to her husband, 'I know this man who often comes our way is a holy man of God. Let us make a small room on the roof and put in it a bed and a table, a chair and a lamp for him. Then he can stay there whenever he comes to us.'
>
> 2 Kings 4:8-10

## Your Heart Is Judged By Where You Put Your Treasure

This unnamed woman had a giving heart and she knew Elisha was a true man of God. She wanted to be a blessing to him, so she added a room onto her home which was a huge undertaking for someone who only came by occasionally. She did not do this to be noticed by others, her motive was a love for the purpose and servants of God.

> All man's ways seem innocent to him, but motives are weighed by the Lord.
>
> Proverbs 16:2

> For where your treasure is, there your heart will be also.
>
> Matthew 6:21

When Elisha went up to his room he asked his servant Gehazi what he could for the woman for showing him such kindness. When he called the Shunamite woman up to the room she did not ask for anything. This is the attitude we all should have when we do things to advance the kingdom and purposes of God. When you give your resources, time or expertise, do it with a pure heart and not the motive of giving just so you can receive something in return. Later, his servant informed Elisha that the woman did not have any sons and Elisha called her up and said to her:

> 'About this time next year', Elisha said, 'you will hold a son in your arms.'
>
> 2 Kings 4:16a

When you focus on the work of God's kingdom He will bless you with the deep desires of your heart. It may however require faith to receive a blessing that you have convinced yourself is not possible. This woman knew that her husband was old, and the thought of bearing children was buried deep in her heart. She was so convinced it could not happened she tried to stop the prophet from blessing her.

> 'No my lord,' she objected, 'Don't mislead your servant, O man of God!' But the woman became pregnant and the next year about that same time she gave birth to a son, just as Elisha had told her.
>
> 2 Kings 4:16b-17

# The Master Motivator

Love is the master motivator for conceiving your dream and giving birth to your vision, because it takes the focus off of you and puts it on the purposes of God. That is why the Bible says that faith is expressed through love (Galatians 5:6), because we who have been forgiven much should love that much more (Luke 7:47). This woman knew it was a privilege for her to bless a true prophet of God; but her primary desire was to give. One of the ways you can conceive your dream and give birth to your vision is to help someone else accomplish theirs. The woman was wealthy but she did not try to buy her way into a blessing. She saw someone advancing the work of the Lord, and because of her love for God she gave of her substance. That is why Jesus said:

> But seek first his kingdom and his righteousness
> and all these things will be given to you as well.
> Matthew 6:33

God's focus is on expanding his kingdom on earth. You must receive a revelation of that and shift your focus to advancing the kingdom of God as well. God will pour out blessings to fulfill your deepest desires because He knows you will use them for His glory. It would be unwise to try and pick and choose whom you are going to bless based on how you feel about an individual. That is not the kind of example that God gave us to follow. You should not be in the habit of only blessing other Christians or people who think like you. That is the mistake most of the body of Christ is making today. God wants the vision that is being birthed through to bless all of His creation.

For God so loved the **world** that he gave his one and only Son, that whoever believes in him shall not perish but have eternal life. For God did not send his Son into the **world** to condemn the **world,** but to save the **world** through him.

John 3:16-17

But God demonstrated his own love for us in this: While we were still sinners, Christ died for us.

Romans 5:8

When you are in the process of giving birth to your vision and even after it manifest, use it to be a blessing to others as the Spirit of God leads you. Allow the love that is in you help your vision to expand. That love motivates God's favor in your life because His heart is turned toward all of his creation and not just Christians.

Do not be surprised if, for your acts of kindness, the enemy attacks you. As the story of the Shunamite woman continues her son dies from what may have been a heat stroke. But her faith led her back to the prophet and her son was brought back to life. When your vision suffers an attack, remember to have faith in God who gave you the vision and you can overcome any obstacle.

You have the master plan of redemption, with the master key of worship along with the master motivator of love. You know the heart of God and the will of God, and with love in your heart you are ready to pray for his will to be fulfilled in your life.

This is the confidence we have in approaching God; that if we ask anything according to his

will, he hears us. And if he hears us—whatever
we ask—we know we have what we ask of him.
1 John 5:14-15

Pray in faith for God to reveal or confirm your vision.
After you have received your answer, you are ready to learn
how to protect your conception before using it to help build
the kingdom.

Part V

# NURTURE and PROTECT

# CHAPTER ELEVEN
## Hidden Treasure

I CANNOT RECALL a time that I have been invited to someone's home so they could show me where they keep their valuables. They would be aware that I knew they had valuables, but they did not think it would be wise to give me the location of the diamonds and family heirlooms. I may even see those items being worn at a dinner party, but they will eventually be put back into their hiding places. When you walk into your bank you do not get a guided tour of the vault. *Even the pens are secured with metal chains!* You must learn to value and protect what is developing inside of you and in like manner protect your tangible assets. You must make sure there is never any unauthorized access to your conception.

In the book of Luke chapter one, we find a priest named Zechariah and his wife Elizabeth. They were gracious people who had served the Lord with sincerity yet they never conceived a child. Because Elizabeth was barren she suffered the humiliation of having a husband who faithfully served in the temple, yet she did not produce an heir to continue the family legacy. While Zechariah was ministering in the temple and praying an angel of the Lord appeared to him.

> When Zechariah saw him he was startled and gripped with fear. But the angel said to him: 'Do not be afraid, Zechariah; your prayer has been

heard. Your wife Elizabeth will bear you a son
and you are to give him the name John. He will
be a joy and a delight to you, and many will
rejoice because of his birth.'

Luke 1:12-14

Even as an old man Zechariah was still praying for a
son, now his answer had finally come. The angel declared
that the child would be a Nazirite who would lead his
people back to God. How did Zechariah react to his
answered prayer? Like you may have responded in your
previous experiences, he did not believe.

Zechariah asks the angel, 'How can I be sure of
this? I am an old man and my wife is well along
in years.'

Luke 1:18

Think about it, Zechariah prayed for a son and God sent
an angel to the temple to proclaim it. However, the one
who prayed for the miracle does not believe. Because of his
unbelief and the fact that he asked for a sign the angel
caused him to become mute. That is the condition he was in
when he returned to his wife. I believe God had the angel
take away his ability to speak so that he could not go home
and spread that unbelief to his wife when God was about to
bless her. When God moves you away from those whose
words have great influence on your life, do not go running
after them. It may be that God has removed them from your
life for a season so that you will only listen to Him.

Now after those days his wife Elizabeth
conceived; and she hid herself five months,

saying, 'Thus the lord has dealt with me, in the days He looked upon me, to take away my reproach from among my people.'

Luke 1:24-25 (NKJV)

It is important to understand why she hid herself. She was carrying in her womb the same thing you should carry in your spirit. Your conception, no matter what it may be, must ultimately proclaim the good news of the kingdom of God and lead people to Jesus Christ. Zechariah was operating in unbelief so his ability to speak death to his wife's vision was taken from him before she conceived. Elizabeth secluded herself to protect the precious life that was growing in her. The Greek word used for her hiding or seclusion is *perikruptos*, which means to hide from the external and internal environmental influences. Elizabeth knew the blessing that was inside of her needed to be nurtured until it was mature. This was her miracle baby and she was not about to lose him. You must protect your vision in the same manner because what God has placed in you is too precious to be exposed to the world before it is mature. Elizabeth was also being prepared to help her young cousin Mary, the mother of Jesus.

The Bible says that in the sixth month of Elizabeth's pregnancy, Mary came to Elizabeth. When Mary arrived, Elizabeth's baby, who was to be John the Baptist, leaped in his mother's womb. John grew up and proclaimed the way to repentance and salvation, and I pray that your vision will do the same. John's preaching led many people to Jesus and I pray that whatever arena that your vision calls you to, whether business, politics, education or any other area, does the same. Protect your conception; the outcome of someone's eternal destiny may be depending on you.

# CHAPTER TWELVE
## Growing Spiritually to Support Your Vision

BE ENCOURAGED that at this point that if you have yet to conceive your dreams, you are ready to do so now. As I stated earlier a womb is best suited to carry a vision when it is mature. With that in mind let us take a look at some characteristics that will help you to mature so that your vision can come to fruition. Peter writes:

> For this very reason, make every effort to add to your faith goodness; and to your goodness knowledge; and to knowledge, self-control; and to self-control, perseverance; and to perseverance, godliness; and to godliness, brotherly kindness; and to brotherly kindness, love.
>
> 2 Peter 1:5-7

You have received God's divine nature through salvation and the indwelling of His Spirit. You have the ability to live in a way that is pleasing to God. All of the qualities described in the previous verses help you to mature in the Lord. You have the faith to believe the word of God, and by adding each of these traits you are strengthening your spirit to carry your God-inspired vision. Why do you need faith? Because that is how God operates. Why do you need to possess goodness? So you can carry out your vision with excellence. Knowledge is needed to help you do things right the first time and self-control makes sure you stay on track because:

> Where there is no revelation the people cast off restraint (discipline).
>
> Proverbs 29:18

You need perseverance to keep going during the lean times and the struggles in life. Godliness is needed to reflect the image of your creator and brotherly kindness is necessary to let your fellow man know you desire to be a blessing to him. Finally love is necessary because that is the essence of God.

> For if you possess these qualities in increasing measure, they will keep you from being ineffective and unproductive [**barren and unfruitful NKJV**] in your knowledge of our Lord Jesus Christ.
>
> 2 Peter 1:8

Purpose in your heart to be Christ-like; your spiritual maturity has a direct effect on the development of your vision.

# CHAPTER THIRTEEN
# How to Discover Your Vision and Write It Down

I WANT TO ENCOURAGE YOU and help you realize that writing your vision down is not as difficult or complicated as many of you may believe. However, is necessary to plan out what you want to do to make sure you are not wasting time and resources. Everyone has *good* ideas that inspire them and things they think about pursuing from time to time. It is important that you understand that the idea(s) that linger and continue to come back need to be nurtured. God is the source of all the great things you desire to accomplish and "being confident of this, that he who began a good work in you will carry it on to completion until the day of Christ Jesus" (Phil. 1:6).

When seeking to discover your purpose and fulfill your vision you must learn to distinguish some key elements. You must understand the difference between what is **good** and what is **right.** You may get many *good* ideas, but that does not mean they are *right* for you. Good ideas come and go, ideas from God persist. Good ideas can be adopted from other people's work and activities, but the right idea comes from God and is for you alone. This type of idea is always in agreement with God's word. You must exercise confidence the inner calling that speaks to you. In the secular arena as well as the spiritual there are key questions that almost all humans ask themselves.

1. **Who am I?** This is a question that addresses identity. Reading Ps 139:13-18 will provide key insights to your identity, especially where it states to be encouraged that God created you to be exactly what He wanted. This is an amazing truth, your gender ethnicity and all other factors were designed by God for a purpose. We are His workmanship and were created to do good works that have been ordained by Him.

2. **Where am I from?** You can tell a great deal about something when you are aware of its source. If we are merely just another animal or creature that has no specific origin then our desire to accomplish anything would be meaningless. However, you must internalize the reality that you come from God (Gen. 1:28). The real you, your spirit, was called out from Him and your connection to God is your eternal ancestry.

3. **Why am I here?** Now we come to the real reason for all of our existence. Two of those reasons are for God's good pleasure (Rev. 4:11) and to do good works (Eph. 2:10). It is a question that we all need to know as individuals, because as Solomon concluded, to have life and not know why is more frustrating then never experiencing a full life (Ecc. 6:1-5). Because you know you were created to do good works, identifying and achieving them will be your greatest source of fulfillment.

4.  **What can I do?** You must be aware of your potential
    and be willing to work to manifest the deep riches of
    it. We often know or read about people with
    untapped gifts that they squander through poor
    decisions, yet we fail to acknowledge that most of us
    are guilty of the same error. Whatever God has
    given you the ability to do will not just happen. You
    must identify your abilities and work to maximize
    them. As the scripture states: *"Whatever your hand
    finds to do, do it with all your might, for in the realm
    of the dead, where you are going, there is neither
    working nor planning nor knowledge nor wisdom"*
    (Ecc. 9:10). We often believe that finding our
    purpose is some big mystery that God must send us a
    sign or some mysterious event must occur. The truth
    of the matter is that when you are in a right
    relationship with God, your mind will reveal the
    truth of your purpose. The word declares, "The
    plans of the righteous are just" (Pr. 12:5a). When
    you are seeking the purposes of God and the will of
    God for your life, your thoughts or *ideas* are right.
    God is powerful enough that if you sway off track he
    can get you back on the right path.

5.  **Where am I going?** This is the final question and
    your pursuit of an answer is fueled by your desire to
    reach a destination. While pursuing the answer, you
    must internalize that your relationship with God
    compels you to reach far beyond the scope of what
    you can do in your own strength. As the scripture
    says, *"Now to him who is able to do immeasurably*

*more than all we ask or imagine, according to his power that is at work within us"* (Eph.: 3-20). Whatever you plan to do and wherever you want to go, God's plans are bigger. If you want to do great things, then think big.

## The Revelation of Vision

No matter how big your vison is God will do *immeasurably more* than you can imagine. Knowing the answers to these questions will bring a boldness to your spiritual walk and your faith will be fortified in its certainty that your vision will be realized. You must have confidence in the things your mind is showing you. That is how God operates. He shows you what He will do if you are willing to trust Him. Having a vison about your future is not affiliated to some mystic religion as some have erroneously concluded. God uses your imagination to take you beyond where you are to where you can be. So many people never do anything because they are afraid they will *miss God* and fail.

Failure is a part of success. Failure is a part of success. That is not a typo—you need to make sure you internalize that. Even when things do not work in the way you have planned them to you can learn from your mistakes. Some things can be avoided as "Plans fail for lack of counsel, but with many advisers they succeed" (Pr. 15:22). However if you never attempt anything great you will definitely fail. Trust what God is showing you.

Look at how God worked in times past for a man who had no children in his old age: "After this, the word of the Lord came to Abram in a vision" (Gen. 15:1). God gave

Abram a picture of his future, "He took him outside and said, "Look up at the sky and count the stars—if indeed you can count them." Then he said to him, "So shall your offspring be." (Gen 15:5). That's immeasurably beyond his and our imagination. God spoke to Abraham's grandson Israel: "And God spoke to Israel in a vision at night and said, "Jacob! Jacob!"(Gen 46:2). You never ask God to give you a vision; this type of request can open the door to deception. God will reveal the greatness he has planned for you and it will come when you choose to be obedient to His call. This is not some mysterious event; it can be as simple as a persistent idea that continues to grow and expand. Remember whatever you see should never contradict God's word. If it does, it is not from God.

## Writing the Vision Down

You will continue to see the vison of your life in your mind; however, taking the additional step to write it down will help you to move from concept to action. When architects oversee the construction of building they have designed, they always have a copy of the blueprint. In the same manner, you should seek to have a blueprint for your life. There are steps you can take to complete this process.

1. Decide what you truly are passionate about. Exercise your faith to believe "The plans of the righteous are just" (Pr.: 12-5a). This will bring order to what are attempting to do. The word states, "Where there is no revelation, people cast off restraint" (Pr.: 29-18a).

You do not start construction on a house with the roof, it is always with the foundation. As you write you will be able to reference the key areas of the vision you seek to fulfill with limited distractions.

2.   Writing your vision down will help to separate the good ideas from the right ideas. You must remember that God is expecting you to make plans. He gave you imagination and the ability to make your own decisions. If you want God to move you have to move:

> To humans belong the plans of the heart, but from the Lord comes the proper answer of the tongue. All a person's ways seem pure to them, but motives are weighed by the Lord. Commit to the Lord whatever you do, and he will establish your plans. (Pr.: 16:1-3)

You make the plans, and God will show you how to do it. He is interested in your motives: is this for His glory or for yours? When you commit your vision to Him the revelation of how to proceed will come. You may say, "How do I know this is what to do?" Some key principles are that you will have a natural desire to do it, you are inspired by it and it will help others. Remember that when you get off track, God will bring you back to where you need to be.

When I was an undergraduate I studied Business Administration. One of the key principles I was taught was that a successful business always had a mission or purpose statement. This is what the company wanted people to say about it and it activities. As an example Chic Fil A®'s mission statement is "To glorify God by being a faithful steward of all that is entrusted to us and to have a positive influence on all who come into contact with Chick-fil-A." You should make a personal mission statement for your life.

1. The next step you need to take in this is process is establishing goals. It has been stated that a goal is a dream with a deadline. Goals serve as check points for your progress and can also encourage you to continue on the path you have started. You should have both short term and long term goals, and put a date on when each should be completed. This has a psychological effect that allows you to maintain a consistent pace.

2. You also need to write down your values and the things you are not willing to compromise. This will protect your integrity and help you to stand firm when temptation to take short cuts or act unethically comes.

3. Assess your strengths and weakness and write them down. This will help determine what you can do on your own, and what you will need others' help to do. Remember you have a personal vision, but that does not mean you do it all by yourself.

## Narrow Your Focus

For some it is very difficult to narrow down their activities. They are convinced they must do everything.

Others think that if they don't work on multiple projects they are somehow missing out on something. When you and your vision are continuously vacillating you will constantly change what you are believing God for, and as James says: *"Such a person is double-minded and unstable in all they do."* You need to make a decision to do what is most important and stick to it.

When you seek to do everything you also have the tendency to procrastinate, which is a very interesting word: *Pro* means "forward" and *Crastinus* means "belonging to tomorrow." When you are properly focused you will do what needs to be done. Busy does not equal effective and your vision cannot prosper on a merry-go-round.

You will have seasons in your life where you will do different things, but as Paul stated, "Brethren, I do not regard myself as having laid hold of it yet; but **one** thing I do: forgetting what lies behind and reaching forward to what lies ahead, I press on toward the goal for the prize of the upward call of God in Christ Jesus" (Phil: 3-13-14).

Paul had done terrible things in the name of God during a particular time in his life that he originally believed were good things. He did not try to go back and fix everything or spend his days trying to make up for it; he moved forward. You don't consult your past to determine your future. Do not allow what you did not do before to distract from achieving the thing you desire to accomplish now. Stay focused on the revelation God has given you, and give birth to the vison of your heart.

# Taking Action

It is my prayer that you have been inspired to dream big even if you are sleeping in a small bed. God has great treasure invested in you, but only you have the key to open it up and share it with the world. To every mother who reads this book, remember that there is no greater calling than motherhood. To everyone who has fallen short of a lofty goal, consider that the difference between success and failure is getting up one more time. To every woman who has been frozen with fear, just take one step of faith; the difference between water that flows and ice is only one degree.

1.  Ask God to reveal or confirm your vision; He is the only one who can validate what you see in your spirit. Remember that He is the one who placed the dream in your heart and even if your dream has been buried under years of frustration and distraction, God can bring back to the forefront of your mind.

2.  When you conceive it, protect it. Everyone who acts as if they have your best interests at heart does not. You need to learn to discern when to disclose the plans that you have for your future. You must protect your dream from the destructive words, attitudes, and habits of people who do not respect the gift in you.

3.  Write the vision down (Habakkuk 2:2-3). Any plans you make that are not on paper are just plans. They will remain a dream and never become a reality. If anyone desires to construct a building, the city

requires that they present a blueprint of what they intent to build. They must show on paper what they desire to do on the land. You should treat your vision with the same respect. You can always adjust the blueprint. However, without a written plan, if conditions change, you have no point of reference that you can use to adjust your plans.

4.  Follow the leading of the Holy Spirit. The Spirit of God is your guide. He will lead you to the places you need to go and the people you need to meet. Do not expect everything He tells you to do to agree with your logic. Trust Him and He will bring you to your place of blessing.

5.  Be willing to give up unprofitable activities or relationships to achieve your dream as the scripture says, "Turn my eyes away from worthless things; preserve my life according to your word (Ps. 119:37). The word says what does it profit a man if he gains the whole world and loses his soul? No one will be with you when you stand before God and give an account of what you did with your life. You cannot afford to let someone or something get in the way of your destiny. To whom much is given much is required and that should be enough to convince you your that dream is too valuable to compromise.

You may have heard people use the acronym P.U.S H. to mean pray until something happens. I like the acronym but I would also suggest that you P.U.S H. your vision out during delivery and that means, Pregnancy Unleashes Supernatural Help. If you will receive, conceive, and pursue your vision, you can be assured God will get involved and your vision will come to fruition. The next step is up to you, the fact that you have taken the time to read this book is evidence that you desire to live out your calling. Continue on that path and bless the world with what God has placed in your heart.

## CLOSING THOUGHTS
# The Greatest Conception of All

A LITTLE TEENAGED GIRL received a message from God. She was told she would give birth after conceiving by the Spirit of God. Her response, *may it be unto me as you have said* (Luke 1:38), was the most important conception of all. If you have never done so, I encourage you to consider receiving Jesus Christ into your life. There is no greater decision and no greater joy.

www.ingramcontent.com/pod-product-compliance
Lightning Source LLC
Chambersburg PA
CBHW061147040426
42445CB00013B/1595